Fresher Styles for Web Designers

More Eye Candy from the Underground by Curt Cloninger

New Riders

VOICES THAT MATTER™

Fresher Styles for Web Designers
More Eye Candy from the Underground
Curt Cloninger

New Riders
1249 Eighth Street
Berkeley, CA 94710
510/524-2178
510/524-2221 (fax)

Find us on the Web at www.newriders.com.

To report errors, please send a note to errata@peachpit.com.

New Riders is an imprint of Peachpit, a division of Pearson Education

Project Editor: Rebecca Gulick
Editor: Jill Marts Lodwig
Production Editor: Hilal Sala
Compositor: Kim Scott, Bumpy Design
Indexer: Jack Lewis
Cover Designers: H I T Studio (Lina Grumm and Annette Lux)
Interior Designer: Mimi Heft

ISBN 13: 978-0-321-56269-2

ISBN 10: 0-321-56269-0

9 8 7 6 5 4 3 2 1

Printed and bound in the United States of America

For my children, Caroline, Jordan, Robin, and James.
God has marvelous plans for you—plans to prosper you and
not to harm you, plans to give you hope and a future.
Y'all are precious to me and I couldn't be any prouder.

Acknowledgments

Thanks to everybody who worked on this book. Special thanks to my editor Jill Marts Lodwig who kept the book from becoming an academic treatise while still allowing it to be clever. Thanks to my colleagues and students in the Multimedia Arts & Sciences department at UNC Asheville for perpetually challenging and inspiring me. Thanks to my wife, Julie, for being so freaking sexy. Finally, thanks to all the designers and artists whose work is featured in this book. You make the web a place I still want to be.

Contents

THERE'S A DESTINATION
A LITTLE UP THE ROAD

FROM THE HABITATIONS
AND THE TOWNS WE KNOW

A PLACE WE SAW THE LIGHTS
TURN LOW

JIGSAW JAZZ AND THE
GET-FRESH FLOW

—BECK

01 | FRESHER STYLES FOR A CHANGING WEB

In 2001, I wrote a book called *Fresh Styles for Web Designers: Eye Candy from the Underground*. At the time, the dot-com bubble was still relatively intact, bandwidth had increased enough to make Macromedia Flash a viable web design option, and wars were raging in the web design community over which best practices would prevail. Would the web become a minimal, text-centric channel of efficient information delivery (the web as database interface model), or would it become a high-bandwidth interactive entertainment channel (the web as interactive TV model)? I argued that the web would become both of these things and a dozen more that we could not yet envision, and of course it has.

During this time, I proposed that 10 design styles (**Figures 1.1** through **1.10**) were pushing web design beyond the conservative, duotone, brochure-ware approach of most corporate web sites. These styles ranged from the hyper-conservative HTMinimaLism (**Figure 1.8**) to the hyper-anarchic Pixelated Punk Rock (**Figure 1.6**).

Figure 1.1 Gothic Organic style (entropy8.com)

Figure 1.2 Grid-Based Icon style (hoggorm.anart.no/)

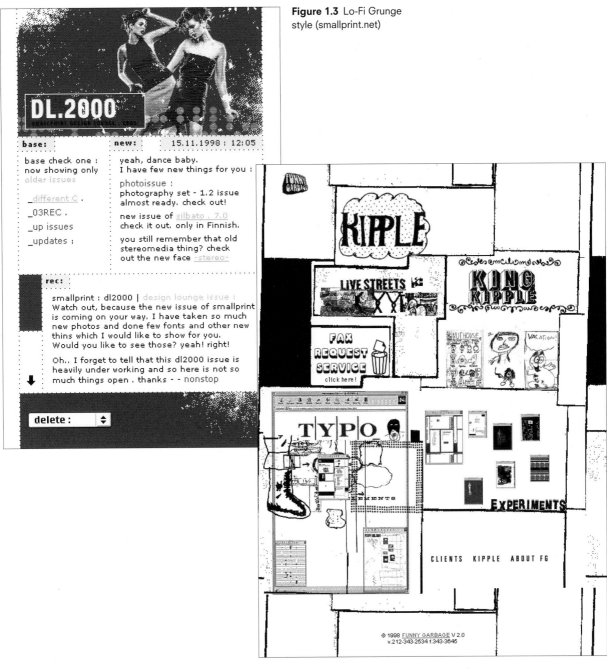

Figure 1.3 Lo-Fi Grunge style (smallprint.net)

Figure 1.4 Paper Bag style (funnygarbage.com)

Figure 1.5 Mondrian Poster style (once-upon-a-forest.com)

Figure 1.6 Pixelated Punk Rock style (titler.com)

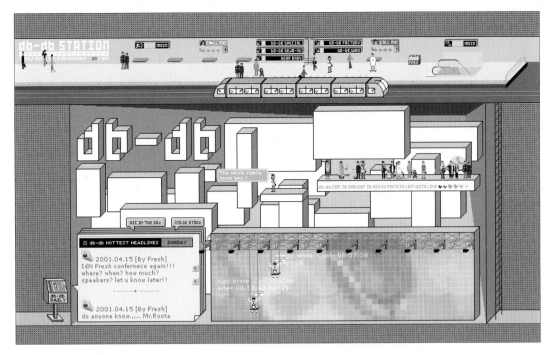

Figure 1.7 SuperTiny SimCity style (db-db.com)

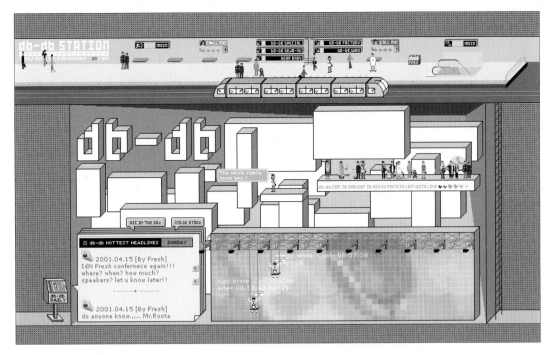

37signals

25 Just Because You Can, Doesn't Mean You Should

Light type, dark background

Scrolling news ticker

Spinning logo

Frames

Beveled Buttons

Pictures of the executive team

Splash page

Music

Bar down the left side

Putting your brochure online

Banner ads

3D

Virtual reality

None of these things are inherently bad. There is no evil in any one of them. The problem is that many of these things are used because they can be rather than because they should be.

Sure, there are times when light type on a dark background is appropriate, but we don't think "it just looks cool" is reason enough.

37signals believes that "hip" and "legible" don't have to be mutually exclusive. We love "cool" as much as the next person, but we also realize that part of our job is to make people's lives easier, not harder.

Other Signals

37 HOME000102030405060708091011121314151617181920212223242526272829303132333435363 7PORTFOLIOCONTACT ≪ ≫

Figure 1.8 HTMinimaLism style (37signals.com)

Figure 1.9 Drafting Table/Transformer style (designgraphik.com)

Figure 1.10 1950s Hello Kitty style (atlasmagazine.com)

Over the ensuing years, XHTML and Cascading Style Sheet (CSS) standards have enabled the HTMinimaLism approach to become a default standard for blog design. Meanwhile, further increases in bandwidth and a curatorial turn away from conceptualism and toward pop art have spawned a scene of Pixelated Punk Rock Internet artists, willfully celebrating the indulgences of intentional browser crashing and fullscreen animated .gif chaos (**Figure 1.11**).

Some of these original 10 styles, including Gothic Organic and Mondrian Poster, proved readily adaptable to a variety of commercial and personal online design uses. Other styles were either too idiosyncratic to widely proliferate, such as 1950s Hello Kitty, or simply got chewed up and discarded as popular styles evolved (think Drafting Table Transformer and Lo-Fi Grunge).

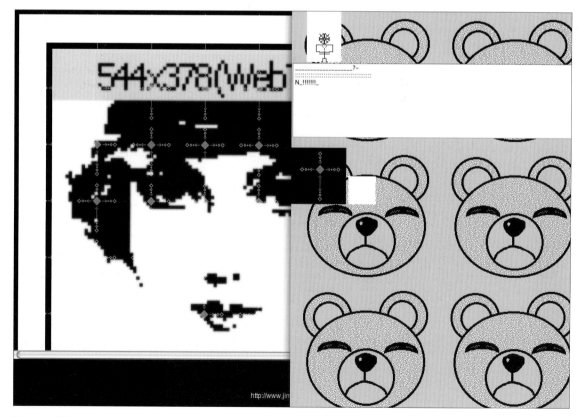

Figure 1.11 jimpunk.com

In 2005, I was invited to write a sequel to *Fresh Styles*, but I declined because it didn't seem like enough had changed in the world of web design to constitute a batch of entirely new styles. But now, in 2008, the time is right for this book.

The web itself has changed significantly, not just in its appearance but also in its function. Everyday people who used to go online to visit other people's web sites now go online to update their own. Web designers aren't the only people making sites. And the proliferation of blogs and social networking sites has changed the face of the web and the ground rules of web design.

Now that your client can design a passable looking site for free, you must offer something more than a passable looking site. Sometimes your added value is in branding, consulting, and strategizing, but often it is in customization and specialization—providing a look and function that not only suits your client's business, but also distinguishes your client's site from all the other template-generated cookie-cutter sites on the web.

Now more than ever, commercial designers need fresher styles. Like *Fresh Styles for Web Designers*, this book examines several styles that will hopefully inspire you to design unique, appropriate, distinctive, nongeneric, value-added sites.

Why Stir Things Up Again?

Now that web standards are finally standard, now that blog templates allow anyone to make a decent looking web page, and now that web designers are finally gaining their standing in the design community as professionals—why come in with a bunch of unorthodox, Mickey-Mouse design approaches that haven't been user-tested, commercially-validated, or corporately-approved? Lots of reasons:

- As the technical specifications of the medium evolve, several of our current best design practices become inapplicable. For instance, so much was made over the separation of CSS style and XHTML content because of the advent of mobile computing devices. We were soberly warned, "The web of your handheld device will *not* look like the web of your computer monitor." Then Apple came out with the iPhone interface, and suddenly the web of our handheld device looked strikingly similar the web of our computer monitor. Of course, separation of CSS style and XHTML content is still a good idea, but not necessarily for the reasons that had been proposed.

- Experimental design itself evolves the medium, suggesting prototypical uses of hardware, software, and protocols that have not yet been standardized. It leads to better uses of the Internet, better ways of communicating, and better ways of being in the world.

```
            'Fury said to a
            mouse, That he
        met in the
    house,
    "Let us
  both go to
  law: I will
    prosecute
        you. – Come,
            I'll take no
                denial; We
                    must have a
                    trial: For
                    really this
                    morning I've
                    nothing
                    to do."
                Said the
                mouse to the
                cur, "Such
                a trial,
            dear Sir,
        With
      no jury
      or judge,
    would be
    wasting
      our
        breath."
            "I'll be
                judge, I'll
                    be jury "
                    Said
                    cunning
                    old Fury:'
                    "I'll
                    try the
                    whole
                    cause,
                    and
                condemn
            you
            to
            death."
```

Figure 1.12 *"The Mouse's Tale" from Lewis Carroll's* Alice in Wonderland, *1865*

- As a new medium, interactive design is inherently experimental. For avant-garde writers like Stéphane Mallarmé, the Futurists, the concrete poets, and the Oulipo, typesetting was inherently experimental. It became an artistic hybrid between poetic text and painterly space (**Figure 1.12**). Web design further hybridizes this already hybridized medium of typesetting by adding interaction in the context of a social network. We may fall into the habit of taking the web for granted, but it is still a place of great experimental communicative possibility.

- It's better to have too many design tools than too few. Since 2001, the web has continued to be a largely text-centric medium, but this hasn't kept it from also supporting a massive YouTube and podcast culture, numerous subscription MP3 services, Skype, and streaming HD network television programming. As the web becomes increasingly media diverse, web design approaches and paradigms should become increasingly diverse. What was true of the web in 2001 is still true in 2008: One size does not fit all.

- Experimental design is fun. It makes designing sites and surfing sites less boring. Even from a bottom-line marketing perspective, this is not an unimportant consideration.

Permanence vs. Evolution

Is it a failure that web design styles should change in only seven years? On the contrary. It is evidence of a healthy, robust, evolving medium and culture. The word *style* gets a bad reputation from the fashion industry. It has the derogatory connotations of being superficial and inconsequential. *Styles may change, but the truth remains the same.* Yet *style* is merely a way of doing something. As media, clients, products, services, and audiences change, our way of designing for these situations should necessarily change. The fact that styles change is not evidence of fickleness or whimsy. It is simply evidence that a rapidly changing medium (the web) is being rigorously advanced by a group of flexible, culturally current professionals (web designers).

And just because web design styles evolve, this doesn't mean that web-coding standards erode. Interactive design styles and XHTML-CSS design standards are two very different things. A design style is the way in which you use and apply such standards. Indeed, the technical standards of any programming or markup language should be robust enough to support a wide range of design and development styles. Standards of code should not restrict standards of visual or interactive style. When they do, they should be modified and expanded to accommodate the needs of designers and developers.

In other words, the standards work for us; we don't work for the standards.

Web design has been criticized by certain print-centric designers as not having its own canon of great web design work. This lack of a stable canon is taken as proof that there is no great web design work. In fact, web design is inherently ephemeral. Unlike print designers, web designers rarely definitively finish a project. For example, this book is completed, shipped, and printed; but the web site for this book (lab404.com/fresher) continues to be updated (until the next book, or until I get tired of updating it). In other words, web designers are often too busy building 2.0 and 3.0 versions of everything to bother archiving their work for posterity.

True, archive.org keeps an archived backlog of earlier versions of many web sites, but the archived versions are often incomplete and broken. Archivists of web sites can't merely take screenshots of the sites, because web sites are designed for use. A true archivist is interested in how the sites function as well as what they look like. So in essence, web design is inherently more ephemeral than print design.

The problem is not that web design looks bad and is unworthy of archiving, but that the canon of web design is more fluid than the canon of graphic design. This is because the

WEB DESIGNERS ARE OFTEN TOO BUSY BUILDING 2.0 AND 3.0 VERSIONS OF

EVERYTHING TO BOTHER ARCHIVING THEIR WORK FOR POSTERITY.

A Different Approach to Teaching Design

medium itself is more fluid. The history of web design will be archived differently. Its (r)evolution will not be televised.

This book is a collection of website screen shots with accompanying commentary. The screen shots will only partially convey the efficacy of these designs, so I invite you to visit the URLs and surf the sites. See how they function, and how they intuitively "feel" as you use them. And don't be too disappointed if some of the sites aren't there any more. Such is the ephemeral nature of the web.

There are two basic ways to teach design. The first is to teach general fundamental principles, follow them step-by-step, and let the specific visual aesthetics arise from the principles. The second is to show samples and examples—to begin with a bunch of visual examples of work, and then work backward to distill the basic principles. There are plenty of design books that take the step-by-step approach. This book takes the samples and examples approach. Neither approach is better or worse; both should be used in conjunction with each other.

The Myth of Pure Originality

The question inevitably arises: "If I begin by looking at examples of other people's work, how will I ever develop my own original style?" Personally, I think the idea of an original design style is a residual myth from the "artist as hero" era. Nothing comes from a vacuum, nor should it. Choose an artist or design that you deem a "true original" (from Picasso to David Carson). Then dig a little deeper, and you'll discover they were influenced by all sorts of precedents (from African masks to Sex Pistols posters). Being exposed to these styles won't harm your "originality." On the contrary, such exposure will probably improve it.

THE IDEA OF AN ORIGINAL DESIGN STYLE IS A RESIDUAL MYTH FROM THE "ARTIST

AS HERO" ERA. NOTHING COMES FROM A VACUUM, NOR SHOULD IT.

Why Taxonomies?

Why organize these examples of design work into taxonomical categories? Doesn't such pigeonholing and stereotyping ignore the originality of each singular design approach?

This is the inherent problem with any taxonomy. If we never categorized anything, then each blade of grass would be absolutely unique, and we would have billions of kinds of grass (or more accurately, no kinds of grass at all). So we use language to make a distinction between crab grass and monkey grass. These distinctions are admittedly relative, based on characteristics we choose to recognize and ignoring others. Inevitably, there are always exceptions that refuse to cooperate with our taxonomies (for example, the platypus, the virus, and algae).

Taxonomical design categories are useful in that they allow us to recognize similarities, make connections, make distinctions, and judge appropriate uses for various approaches. A well-organized, usefully categorized, appropriately labeled list of sites is more valuable than the same sites in an unordered list. Taxonomical organization allows patterns to emerge and a big-picture perspective to occur. Additional commentary, explanation, and justification make a taxonomy all the more relevant.

The design categories in this book are admittedly relative. They are based on my observations of contemporary web design. I didn't just make them up from scratch, but I did just make them up. Unlike an art historian, I'm not trying to canonize or delineate art movements. I'm simply delineating certain visual styles useful for working designers.

These styles are meant to be inspirational launching pads from which to work. They are starting points, not rigid destinations. They are meant to instigate a creative conversation. Hopefully, they will hybridize and evolve depending on the needs of your particular project.

Is this book the birth of styles that have yet to happen, or simply an account of styles that are already happening? Both. If you launch from these styles, you are already following paths that, if not yet well established, have at least been previously explored. But none of these styles will have occurred in the context and service of your particular project, under your particular guidance. Hopefully this book will coalesce, explicate, and further disseminate better, less sterile, more interesting web design. Whether these styles are ultimately traceable back to this book is wholly immaterial. My goal is to make the web a better (and not simply a more quantifiably functional) place to work, play, live, and be.

The Myth of Function-Driven Design

Why begin with style at all? Why not begin with function? Isn't form supposed to follow function? So goes the modernist mantra, but it is a bit of a myth. Given the function of a chair (to support a sitting person), there are any of number of stylistic forms that "follow" (**Figure 1.13**). All are informed by the basic functional requirements of a chair, but no single style emerges indisputably victorious from the pure, objective, Platonic realm of chairness. Each

Figure 1.13 Same function, different forms

style is a complex amalgam of philosophical concepts, inherited ways of being in the world, inherited ways of working with materials, physical properties of materials, and yes, functional requirements. Modernist styles are no exception (although they often claim to be).

Perhaps the modernist chair designer began with the pure functional requirements of the project and, through rigorous and intuitive insight into the nature of the problem, wound up with a brand new style. Probably not. This is the myth of the heroic artist foisted on the design craftsman. As mentioned above, even the "purest" designers are pulling from a reservoir of things they have seen, experiences they have had, and an overall cultural and historical way of being in the world.

As long as all design must have a style, why not admit it, get over it, and begin understanding contemporary styles? This doesn't mean that you ignore the functional considerations of your project. On the contrary, they should indicate which design styles are most appropriate for your project. The perpetual challenge is to apply each style adaptively, intelligently, and integrally rather than merely slap it (or "skin it") on rotely.

About The Styles

I am banking on the fact that my browser bookmarks are not your browser bookmarks (although some inevitably will be). Hopefully the sites I have chosen are idiosyncratic enough to be refreshing to most commercial web designers, but not so idiosyncratic that they are commercially inapplicable.

The sites in this book are largely technology agnostic. Some are Flash sites; others are XHTML-CSS sites. Some are hand-coded; others are populated by content management systems. Some are large and corporate; others are small and private. The styles in this book are categorized by their visual design rather than their structural implementation.

Three of the eight styles are largely text-centric: Late(st) Modern, Psychedelic Minimalist, Dot Matrix. In the original *Fresh Styles* book from 2001, only one style (HTMinimaLism) was meant specifically for text-heavy sites. This increase in text-centric design styles is a result of the way the web has evolved in conjunction with other media.

With the advent of increased bandwidth, video over the web has become a reality. You can watch HDTV episodes at abc.com, stream Hollywood movies at netflix.com, and, of course, there's YouTube. Rather than decreasing the need for text-heavy web design styles, fullscreen video over the web has instead decreased the novelty of vector-based Flash animation.

Now that streaming animated video is available on the web, most low-bandwidth Flash animation suddenly looks pretty cheesy (except for animations like homestarrunner.com, which are all the more glorious in their intentional low-fi cheesiness).

True, the navigation and branding components of abc.com still need to be designed, but once you're watching this week's episode of

Lost fullscreen, you want those web design elements to disappear from your browser window. Thus web designers are free to be more creative about designing the text-centric web.

Wilder, less text-centric design styles are still appropriate for other tasks on the web, because the web is a huge place with multiple uses. Sometimes design wants to be unobtrusive, and other times it wants to be center stage. For your more obtrusive design needs, Hand-Drawn Analog style and Corkboard Sprawl style should serve well. For your obnoxious, uncalled-for, and irreverently gaudy design needs, 1996 Dirt style is positively "off the chain" (in the parlance of our times).

Certain styles (namely 1970s Dayglow Vector, Dusty Cowboy, and Chrome Sheen) were not included in this book because they are more like surface embellishments that don't affect the more intrinsic elements of site design (navigation, response, architecture, overall metaphor).

1970s Dayglow Vector style is the flowering, ornate, baroque filigree style that currently embellishes every other print and TV ad. Dustly Cowboy style is a Wild West saloon style involving Victorian-era woodblock typography, distressed leather, and lots of maroon. Chrome Sheen style is the brushed gunmetal style that currently adorns apple.com and every other corporate web site (as if the web were one big iTunes interface). Chrome Sheen is actually a marked improvement from its 1996 predecessor, Clunky Button Bevel style, although both styles are still intent on making a virtual interface look like a physical electronic device.

There is nothing wrong with 1970s Dayglow Vector, Dusty Cowboy, and Chrome Sheen. They simply seemed a bit played and a bit too much like mere skins.

Web design is its own animal, inherently different than other forms of design. The styles included in this book make sense on the web. They arose in response to the limitations of the web and are particularly suited for the challenges of web design. Hence the title: *Fresher Styles for Web Designers*.

Avoiding Parochialism and Inbreeding

Many web designers and developers follow web design and development through a relatively narrow bandwidth of the blogosphere. This inevitably leads to a kind of unintentional inbreeding. Certain exemplary sites are referenced and foregrounded, often based on their level of technical accomplishment (XHTML-CSS ingenuity, Ajax functionality, Flash ActionScript wizardry, and standards compliance). One problem with approaching web design from a technical perspective is that the nuances of visual communication get backgrounded, and as a result, taxonomies get formed along technical lines (Flash vs. HTML) rather than visual lines (Late[st] Modern style vs. Psychedelic Minimalist style).

Meanwhile, there is an entire web of great design made by people who have never visited w3c.org. They are new media artists, photographers, curators, experimental print designers, musicians, and (dare I say it) MySpace users. For inspiration, many of these designers are looking to contemporary and noncontemporary fine art, contemporary and noncontemporary experimental print design, retro-album covers, psychedelic concert posters, outdated technological interfaces, and a wealth of pop culture detritus. This book visits and examines some of these less provincial sites with the intention of widening the circle of dialogue around web design.

The subtitle of this book is *More Eye Candy from the Underground*, but it's not entirely accurate. Some of these sites are extremely popular, created by designers who rose from the experimental underground to achieve larger commercial success. Other sites are "underground" to web design culture, but very much above ground to Manhattan art gallery culture. Here, *underground* simply means experimental, innovative, and leading edge. It doesn't even mean "rebellious," since styles like Late(st) Modernism are actually quite conservative.

Many of the sites in this book are from the contemporary art community—a community beyond design, yet still very much related in terms of its interest in visual aesthetics, experimentation, and (for better or worse) fashion. More importantly, contemporary arts organizations are used to thinking conceptually, not just visually. Many of these art world sites are boldly, originally, and ingeniously conceived and designed with a refreshing balance of elegance and playfulness. Such sites appear throughout the book in multiple styles.

Influences, Characteristics, and Uses

Each chapter of this book includes three main sections: Influences, Characteristics, and Uses. The Influences section examines the sources of each style—its precedents and origins—to situate it in a historical context. The Characteristics section examines the current state of each style on the web. I analyze various exemplary sites, elucidating their visual and functional characteristics. Some technical tips and observations are offered, but much of the technology used in the construction of these sites, although not rocket science, is beyond the scope of this "samples and examples" book.

The Uses section suggests possible commercial applications for each style. These applications are by no means prescriptive, but merely suggestions based on prior commercial uses of these styles, and on my own speculative conjecture. How you apply these styles to your commercial projects should ultimately depend on the purpose of your site and the nature of your audience.

● ● ●

There is a wrong-headed argument that if this book becomes popular it will immediately become stale, and you will have to look elsewhere for freshness. That is thinking of style in terms of fashion. Styles are not merely trends, they are "ways of making." Each of these eight styles, these eight ways of making, can be further hybridized, modified, modulated, scaled-down, and reversed. These styles are not ends in and of themselves, but rather a means.

As the web evolves as a medium, web design styles will necessarily co-evolve. It is worth noting that the web never evolves in a vacuum, but always in conjunction with other media. Advances (technological and cultural) in mobile computing are already influencing what the future web will look like. The web's function and use will always be colored by neighboring (and increasingly overlapping) media: telephony, application software, multimedia ROMs, proprietary gaming platforms, TV, radio, CDs, DVDs, public libraries, clothing, architecture, public transit systems. The list is ever increasing and shifting in emphasis. The web will supplement some of these media, supercede others, and meld with others to form new media hybrids. Indeed, it is already doing this.

Still, whatever the web becomes, it will always need to be designed. It will always need to look like something (or several things). As the web evolves in multiple directions, it will increasingly benefit from a multitude of philosophical and stylistic design approaches. Not every one of these styles will be useful to you immediately, but it can't hurt to have some extra styles in your toolbox, for the now and the future web.

I'm Nobody! Who are you?
Are you—Nobody—too?
Then there's a pair of us!
Don't tell! They'd advertise—you know!

How dreary—to be—Somebody!
How public—like a Frog—
To tell one's name—the livelong June—
To an admiring Bog!"

—EMILY DICKINSON

02 | *NO STYLE*

There is no such thing as no style, because everything has a style. A style is simply a "way" of making something, so the only way to have no style is to avoid making something. Even "generic," money-saving products at the grocery store have labels that are designed in a certain style, often incorporating a black-on-white sans-serif typeface that is supposed to represent the fact that no extra marketing or design money was wasted on the production of these labels. In reality, of course, someone is paid to purposefully design labels that best convey the message that the labels have not been purposefully designed.

Hardcore modernist designers like Jan Tschichold thought they could avoid the issue of style by arriving at *the* single correct way of making. Once there is only one correct design style, that style is no longer *a* style, or even *the* style; it simply becomes design itself. Yet at this point in history, modernist-era design has a very recognizable visual style, rightly called *the modernist style*. Oh well.

Influences

This chapter is not about the absence of style, per se, but about a particular kind of style I'm calling *No style*. More radical than simple formal minimalism, No style can be thought of as extreme minimalism to the point of eradicating forms altogether and replacing them with pure ideas and concepts. Of course this approach is impossible, since anything built must have some kind of form. Still, the form of No-style design is meant to seem like nothing but an artifact, a necessary concession to the unavoidable fact that design must assume some contingent form if it is to appear in the world at all.

It's not that No style has no influences. Instead, No-style designers are specifically influenced by the idea of nothing or "no thing." The goal of No-style design is to convey a concept or a body of content as directly as possible, with as little visible design intervention as possible.

No style is not against design intention, but against the visual manifestation of design intention. Ironically, in order to achieve such invisibility of intention, No-style designers have to be inordinately intentional. It is easy enough to make something, and even easier to not make something. But it is quite tricky to intentionally make nothing. No-style designers are not even trying to make something from nothing (magicians do that). Instead, they are trying to make nothing from something. If nothing were something, what would it (not) look like? No-style designers perpetually wrestle with this question.

Such philosophical musings on the paradoxes of nothing are relevant not only to No-style design, but to all design and art. What is the relationship between what something is, what it does, and what it looks like? As an

THE GOAL OF NO STYLE DESIGN IS TO CONVEY A CONCEPT OR A BODY

OF CONTENT AS DIRECTLY AS POSSIBLE, WITH AS LITTLE VISIBLE DESIGN

INTERVENTION AS POSSIBLE. NO STYLE IS NOT AGAINST DESIGN INTENTION,

BUT AGAINST THE VISUAL MANIFESTATION OF DESIGN INTENTION.

interactive designer, how do you decide the appropriate look and behavior of a site based on its content? Does design best serve content by being transparent, or by being overtly but appropriately apparent? Can anything visual, intentional, and purposeful ever be truly transparent? Fortunately, web designers are not the only ones faced with such challenges. Conceptual artists have already given these matters a whole lot of thought (and not for nothing!).

Conceptual Art

Conceptual artists of the 1960s and 1970s were more concerned with the formation of artistic ideas than with the formal craft of their implementation. Much of their art took the form of instructions that could be implemented or not. In his famous Declaration of Intent in 1968, language-based conceptual artist Lawrence Weiner wrote, "1. The artist may construct the piece. 2. The piece may be fabricated. 3. The piece need not be built."[2] In Weiner's mind, each of these approaches have equal weight, since the "art" of the piece is contained in the concept of the piece rather than in any particular implementation.

While Weiner's manifesto may have appeared to let instruction-based conceptual artists off the hook, they still faced a problem: instructions are made up of letters that must be set in a typeface, and there is no such thing as a formless typeface. So in choosing their typefaces, conceptual artists still had to commit to some sort of aesthetic form. They tried sidestepping this problem by choosing the least expressive, most utilitarian typefaces possible, but there is no such thing as a historically generic visual style. So while attempting to avoid expressive style altogether, conceptual art of the '60s and '70s became inescapably associated with a kind of recognizable "unstyle."

According to typographic theorist Johanna Drucker, "Lawrence Weiner's stenciled letters on the wall, as industrial and un-aesthetic as he can make them, or John Baldessari's otherwise-empty 1967 canvas bearing the words 'True Beauty' in block letters are striking instances of self-conscious use of graphical codes. A rough-and-unfussy industrialism, uninflected by the artist's hand, un-expressive of emotion or personal voice, provide[s] the distinctive character to conceptual visual language." Drucker goes on to explain, "No one ever accused conceptual artists or writers of over-doing their graphic design. The under-stated an un-inflected attempt at neutrality is now as formulaic and recognizable-as-code as any other set of graphical principles"[3] (**Figure 2.1**).

No-style designers face a similar challenge: How do you keep the focus off the form and on the concept? This challenge requires ingenious and original conceptual ideas as well as ingenious and original formal design solutions.

Figure 2.1 Lawrence Weiner's "Bits & Pieces Put Together to Present a Semblance of a Whole" (2005). Laser-cut aluminum typography on brick.

Examples

John Cage's 4'33"

John Cage's famous musical composition 4'33"
is a piece in three movements. It lasts for four
minutes and thirty-three seconds (not including interludes between movements), during
which time a pianist sits at a piano but does
not play it. It is properly understood not as a
conceptual one-liner, but as a framing device
that forces the audience to focus their listening on the ambient noises in the room for the
duration of the performance. Cage's conceptual
composition effectively questions the dividing
line between noise and music by framing noise
in order to recontextualize it as music.

4'33" serves as a model for No-style designers, except that instead of framing noise, they
are framing concepts and content.

modernista.com is the quintessential No-style
site, to the point of almost being a nonsite. No
other No-style approach manages to accom-
plish so much conceptually with so little
visually.

Modernista! (the exclamation mark is part
of the brand) is an advertising agency whose
clients include General Motors, Anheuser-
Busch, and Gap. You would think that such a
successful firm would have a visually stunning
portfolio site, and in the past they have. Earlier
iterations of the site read like a laboratory of
twenty-first century experimental web design
(**Figure 2.2**). But in March 2008, modernista.com
boldly went No style and achieved a conceptual
feat that trumped all of their previous visually
innovative versions.

NO-STYLE DESIGNERS FACE A SIMILAR CHALLENGE: HOW DO YOU KEEP THE FOCUS OFF
THE FORM AND ON THE CONCEPT? THIS CHALLENGE REQUIRES INGENIOUS AND ORIGINAL
CONCEPTUAL IDEAS AS WELL AS INGENIOUS AND ORIGINAL FORMAL DESIGN SOLUTIONS.

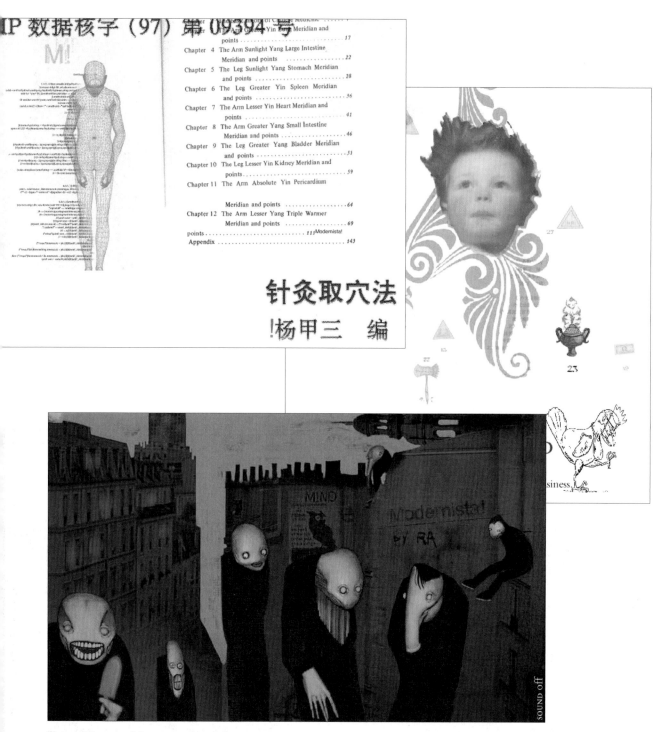

Figure 2.2 modernista.com versions 1–6

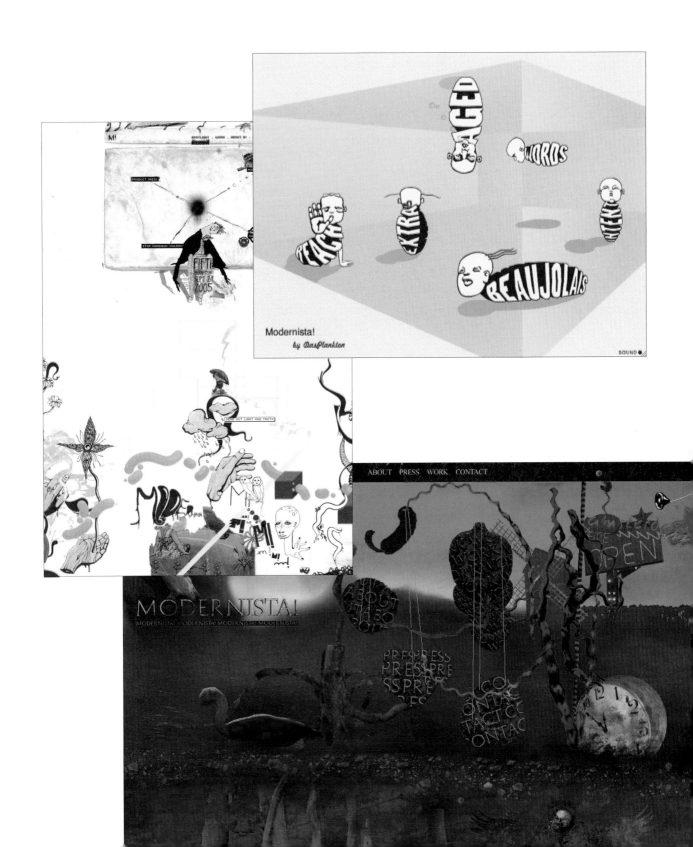

When you link to the current version of modernista.com (version 7) from any other page on the web, the page from which you came appears behind the minimal Modernista! menu (**Figure 2.3**). If you enter "modernista.com" directly into the URL field of a browser, the Wikipedia entry for Modernista! appears behind the Modernista! menu. Its welcome disclaimer reads "You are viewing Modernista! through

the eyes of the web. The menu on the left is our homepage. Everything behind it is beyond our control."

As you scroll through the Modernista! menu, notice that all its portfolio content is hosted on publicly available, "web 2.0" sites. Its print work is on Flickr (**Figure 2.4**), its video work is on YouTube, its web work is linked from del.icio.us, and recent news about the company is found at

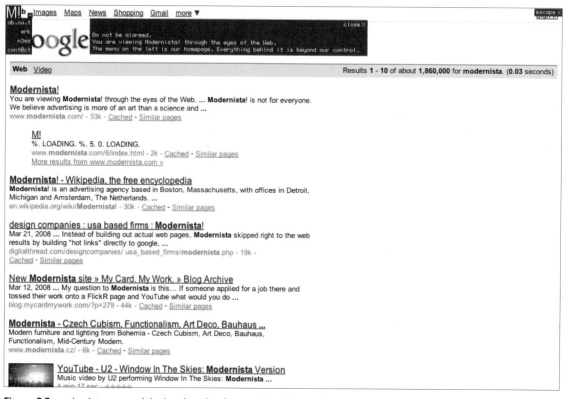

Figure 2.3 modernista.com as it looks when the viewer arrives via google.com

Google News. As you navigate to each of these subsites, the Modernista! menu continues to hover on the top left, uniting these disparate web locations under one very minimalist logo and one very strong conceptual approach. At any time, you can click "escape" on the top right, which removes the menu and lands you at the actual URL of the visible site.

Modernista! achieves No style using the default services of the web that visitors have already absorbed and no longer notice. Each of these sites has its own visual style (because everything has a style), but none of them are designed by Modernista!. So the firm achieves No style via a "not *our* style" conceptual approach.

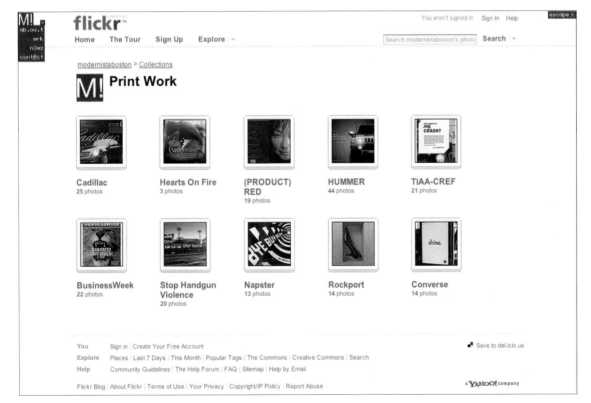

Figure 2.4 modernista.com Flickr subsite

We believe advertising is more of an art than a science and that truly great creative work is priceless in today's cluttered market of parity products.

Our goal is to work with a select group of clients who love and appreciate great advertising as much as we do and who truly want our help building their brand.

Lastly, we wish to create a work environment that fosters responsibility, brilliance and passion, and one that is agile enough to move swiftly in today's business environment.

Figure 2.5 Modernista!'s mission statement

This site is an example of meta-marketers marketing to marketers. Modernista! is not selling products to consumers. It is primarily selling branding services to in-house creative directors at large companies. If I were the creative director of a large company, I would have already seen dozens of slick-looking portfolio sites. I would be looking for something that stands out. After all, if a marketing firm can't distinguish itself amidst the market of other marketing firms, how good will it be at marketing my product? Modernista! conveys simplicity, cleverness, intelligent self-deprecation—and a willingness to sublimate showy design skills so that a stronger concept can emerge. It also adeptly utilizes the existing network.

Of course, if the actual work in Modernista!'s portfolio were mediocre, this conceptual gimmick would backfire. It would seem like its executives chose this novel navigation scheme to cover up the fact that they didn't do very good design work. But the work is extremely strong, and the company's stable of clients is particularly impressive. Because of this, the approach reads like a clever "aw shucks" wink.

To complement the wink, Modernista! menu sections are labeled in an ironic, quasi-hacker, short-form fashion: ab.ou.t, wrk, n3wz, cont@ct.

Its logo is a bitmapped, not even anti-aliased "M." Even its mission statement is terse and to the point, with a bit of self-deprecatingly low-resolution ornamentation added for good measure (**Figure 2.5**). Everything about Modernista!'s approach lets us know that they *could* have built a more ornate portfolio site had they wanted to.

No-style design works so well in this case because Modernista! is selling a service—a kind of fluid, adaptable, intelligent agency that is not wed to any single stylistic solution, but instead monitors the pulse of contemporary culture in order to sell more products to consumers. It is a risky conceptual move that has already paid off for the company in terms of positive press and increased brand recognition.

Indexhibit: A Tool for Transparency

While many web site creation tools use templates that overtly enforce a specific visual style, Indexhibit specifically enforces No style. Indexhibit is a "mini-content management system" that allows anyone to create and maintain an online gallery. The layout template of the software is very simple: On the left side of the page is a vertical menu that acts as an index for the works in the gallery, and on the right side is the exhibit space where the actual work is featured.

The genius of Indexhibit is that it only does what it is meant to do, and no more (**Figure 2.6**). Its conceptual approach results in a lot of white space, an embracing of vertical and horizontal scroll bars, a bare-bones use of typography and color, and a focus on the work being displayed. It is ideal for the display of print design work, since print design already employs its own grid system, color scheme, and typographic approach. The Indexhibit framework simply disappears and refuses to compete with the work being displayed.

The original goal of the Indexhibit project was to get enough designers using this layout "archetype" that the structure would became familiar to the point where visitors no longer notice it and see only the content. While Indexhibit is still wedded to an invisible website format, the software now affords some customization. The artist can add a logo to the top left of the page; different font faces and colors for the menu and body type can be applied; and content can be displayed in a vertical scrolling format, or sequentially via a submenu system.

IF I WERE THE CREATIVE DIRECTOR OF A LARGE COMPANY, I WOULD

HAVE ALREADY SEEN DOZENS OF SLICK-LOOKING PORTFOLIO SITES.

I WOULD BE LOOKING FOR SOMETHING THAT STANDS OUT.

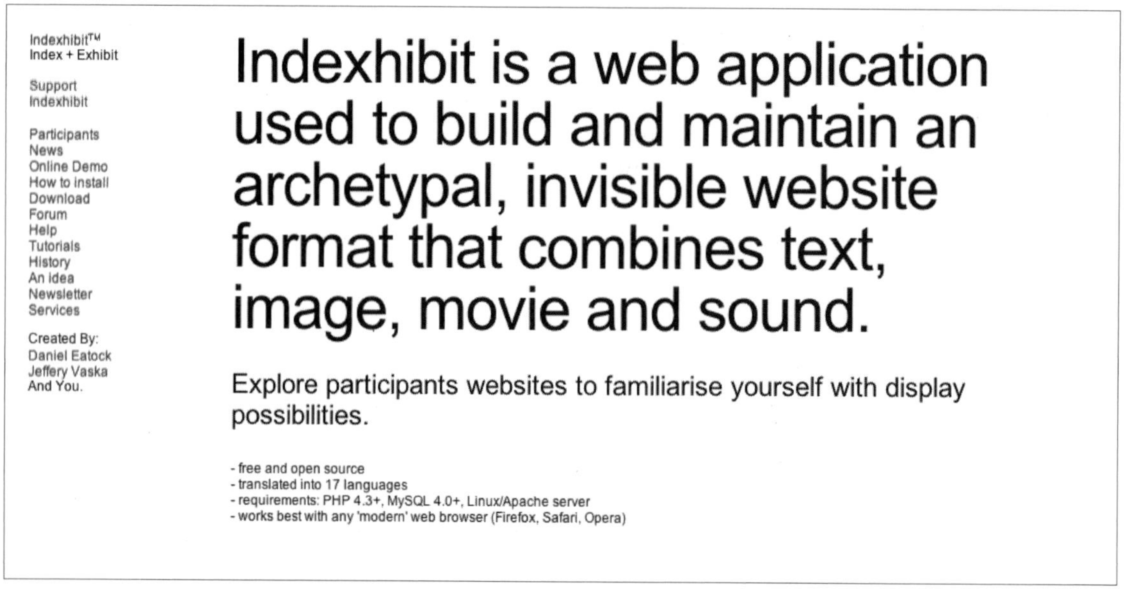

Figure 2.6 indexhibit.com

Regardless how it is customized, the pages still look like an Indexhibit site. Or rather, it's always going to look like a No-style site, since the Indexhibit architecture is purposefully transparent.

When I say that Indexhibit sites look No style, I don't mean that they look generic, unpurposeful, or even old school. Old-school sites from 1996 were based on an entirely different set of defaults: Times New Roman typefaces without any leading, bright blue underlined links, gray backgrounds, and wall-to-wall paragraph text. Most Indexhibit sites tend toward Arial (rather than the more common Verdana), subtle blue links that only reveal underlines when moused over, white backgrounds, and wall-to-wall photographic content with more reasonably constrained text paragraph widths. And all these defaults are customizable.

One old-school trait that Indexhibit sites still retain is a comfortable relationship with vertical scrolling. The left-hand index and right-hand exhibit areas feel and behave like two different frames, but for standards-compliance and browser indexing purposes, they are actually separate HTML divisions (the menu div is set to overflow: auto;, which causes it to scroll vertically if need be). The right-hand exhibit content can scroll vertically while the left-hand index menu remains visible, or vice-versa if there are more menu links than exhibit content. Or both sides can scroll if needed.

To appreciate both the customization that Indexhibit allows and the uniformity of (no) style that it enforces, let's look at a few examples of sites built with Indexhibit.

hit-studio.co.uk is the online portfolio of the firm that designed the cover of this book. Its "logo" on the top left of the page is small, simple HTML text (H I T), and its exhibit format is vertical scrolling, one image on top of the other (**Figure 2.7**).

Photographer Sarah Gerats site is very similar, except that her photographs are larger, taking up more of the exhibit area and giving the portfolio a more full-screen look (**Figure 2.8**).

Mark Reynolds' Indexhibit site has a graphic for a logo, and he has chosen a serif face for his navigation and body text. Instead of vertical scrolling, his exhibit section is divided into subsections for each individual image, with a subnavigation menu at the top of each exhibit (**Figure 2.9**).

Finally, designer Francesca Perani has chosen a magenta and cyan color scheme for her HTMLtext. Her dramatic and playful logo extends the index section further down the page. She has numerous index items, so her index section acquires its own scrollbar. And she too uses submenus for her exhibit sections (**Figure 2.10**).

With each site using the same basic layout template to develop its design, why do they look as unique as they do? Plenty of blogger sites use the same pre-designed blogger template, and they all wind up looking almost exactly the same. The answer has to do with Indexhibit's no-style approach. With Indexhibit, the lion's share of the focus is always going to be on the images displayed in the exhibit section. There is very little extra design intention present. And because every designer's work is different, the sites will always look different.

Indexhibit takes advantage of the well-established convention of left-sided navigation and adds some of its own sensible conventions: a right-sided exhibit area with no limited width, a stationary menu system, CSS-controlled link typography, and unapologetic utilization of horizontal scrolling. It's an ideal No-style model.

Figure 2.7 hit-studio.co.uk

Figure 2.8 sarahgerats.be

MARK REYNOLDS!

An installation based on Vancouver's False Creek. With it's rich and somewhat hidden history, we chose to work with something that is also often hidden, wallpaper. Each layer's pattern represents one aspect of the area's history we uncovered. Featured in *Savfaire Magazine*.

Collaboration with Elicia Di Fonzo.

Prev | Next | 2/4

WORKS
MAKE POP
NO MEANS NO
URBAN PLAN MAGAZINE
ALS PSA
FALSE CREEK WALLPAPER
BURN AND RAZE
MINIATURE PLACES

Built with **Indexhibit**

False Creek Type

Figure 2.9 markreynolds.ca

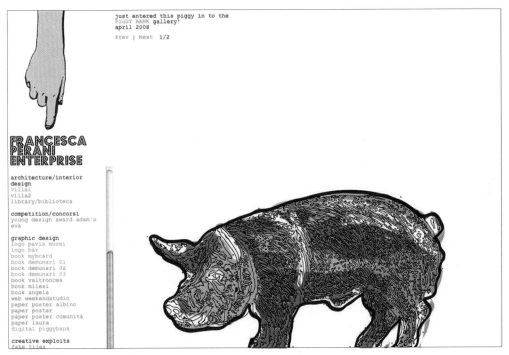

just entered this piggy in to the
PIGGY BANK gallery!
april 2008

Prev | Next 1/2

FRANCESCA PERANI ENTERPRISE

architecture/interior
design
villa1
villa2
library/biblioteca

competition/concorsi
young design award adam'o
eva

graphic design
logo pavia musei
logo bar
book mybcard
book demunari 01
book demunari 02
book demunari 03
book valtroncea
book milesi
book angela
web weekendstudio
paper poster albino
paper poster
paper poster comunità
paper laura
digital piggybank

creative exploits
fake tiles

Figure 2.10 francescaperani.com

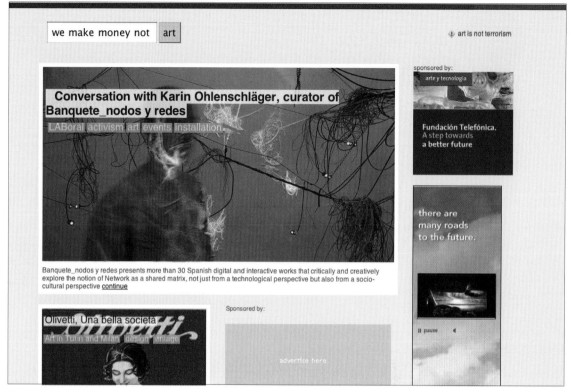

Figure 2.11 we-make-money-not-art.com home page

We Make Money Not Art: The (un)Logo

Régine Debatty's we-make-money-not-art.com is not only one of the hippest contemporary online art news portals, it is also an ingeniously designed web site.

The logo of the site is actually an active search field that turns into a wayfinding device as you browse through the site (**Figure 2.11**). It functions as a kind of un-logo, modifiable by any user, which complements the site's focus on interactive art.

As you enter text in the search field of the logo, the wayfinding button changes to a search button (**Figure 2.12**). Clicking the button initiates a search of the site's content. If you choose to navigate by browsing through sections rather than searching, the logo lets you know what section you are viewing by changing the art button to a design, activism, or architecture button, depending on the section being displayed (**Figure 2.13**).

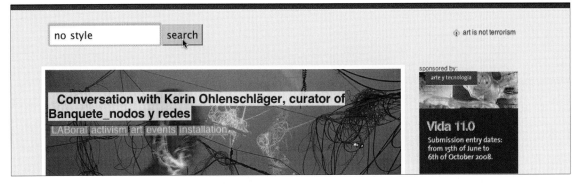

Figure 2.12 we-make-money-not-art.com searchable logo

Figure 2.13 The logo changing to "we make money not design"

A company's logo is traditionally its most sacrosanct element. Corporate color and layout schemes may vary depending on the medium, but the logo treatment almost always remains the same. we-make-money-not-art.com sacrifices control of its logo at the altar of No-style design. The search button is not a .gif image of a search button; it's a giant, HTML search button—a clunky form element from days gone by.

This move says that the site is not about Debatty herself making formally beautiful art (she makes money, remember?), nor is the site about the slickness of its own graphic design (although the site is well designed). Instead, the site is all about the content, its awareness of online history and culture, and its old-school conceptual cleverness. By recontextualizing old-school HTML form elements in an ironic, gigantic way, we make money not art achieves a playful, groovy, and smart version of No-style retro-chic.

Background Killer

A perpetual problem for web designers is how to "kill" background space. Unlike print design, with its known page dimensions, web sites can be any number of sizes depending on the resolution of the surfer's browser. You don't want to fill a 1600-pixel-wide area with wall-to-wall content, since someone viewing from a smaller monitor set at 1000-pixel-wide resolution will have to scroll horizontally to view your content. There are three classic ways to handle the problem of unknown browser width:

- Liquid Layout spreads or shrinks the content percentage-wise based on the width of the browser.

- Jello Layout takes a fixed-width content area and centers it in the middle of the browser (often by placing the content in a division [div] with its left and right margins set to auto). With this solution, the challenge is how to kill the background to the left and right of the content area.

- Ice Layout sets a fixed-width content area flush left in the browser. With this solution, the challenge lies in how to kill the background to the right of the content area.

For the latter two solutions, the default width of the content area (as of 2008) is about 970 pixels wide. This is because the smallest average resolution is 1000 pixels, and browser scrollbars eat up some of that width. So when someone visits your site with a monitor resolution set at 1280 pixels wide, 280 pixels of background space, in addition to your content area, is presented. What to do with this background space?

How do you make it look like it was an intentional part of your design (or at least how do you make it look as if you knew it was going to occasionally be there)? Throughout this book, there will be a "background killer" section for each style, since each style handles this problem in a unique way.

LAB404: DESIGN FRAGMENTS ABSTRACTLY TILED

The default No-style way to kill background space is simply to leave the background white, à la Indexhibit. Nothing says "nothing" like white space. Another, seemingly counter-intuitive solution is to abstract a single visual element from the featured content and tile it repeatedly as the background image. I do this at the current version of my own design portfolio, lab404.com/work (**Figure 2.14**). The result is a kind of nothing from something—an abstract tiling background from a fragment of the foreground content. Decontextualizing and tiling even the subtlest design element always results in unexpected transformations and textures. This simple formal modification can have an inordinately amplified affect.

In the case of my portfolio, the results are fairly overt and baroque, because my own web work tends toward the baroque. But your results needn't be as ornate. Theoretically, since the tiling background design is derived from the foreground content, the user will make a kind of fractal, part-for-the-whole cognitive connection, even if only unconsciously. *Theoretically!*

Figure 2.14 lab404.com/work

Uses

Before beginning any project, you must always decide whether the design should disappear so that the user can better focus on the content, or whether the design should play a more overt role in the user's engagement with the content. The approach you take, of course, depends on the nature of the project.

No style takes the former approach to extremes—the design disappears to the point of invisibility. No-style design is inappropriate for an entertainment site in which the viewer ideally is engaging with the content in a way that augments and brands it. For example, a rock band's site should probably be designed in a style appropriate to the band's music and persona. A movie promotional site should probably be designed in the particular visual style of the movie.

No style is best for content that already has its own design, particularly for design and photography portfolio sites. For instance, if your design portfolio contains work you've done in several different styles, how do you choose the overall style for your portfolio site? If you commit to one style, it will work with certain content, but clash with other content. No-style design solves the problem by staying out of the way altogether and letting each featured piece of visual content speak for itself. No style acts as a kind of invisible frame, focusing attention on the work without attracting attention from it. indexhibit.com even suggests using its template to display not just a collection of design projects, but any kind of collection, such as stamps, records, toys, and so on.

No-style design is also useful for any project in which you want to foreground something other than the design of the site. It seems perfect for an activist site that wants to convey an earnest and urgent tone, focusing on the issues at hand without a lot of frivolities. Unfortunately, many grass-roots sites currently portray their earnestness by being amateurishly designed. No-style design is a way to convey an anti-corporate earnestness while still looking professional.

No style is also perfect for any site that is updated regularly with visual content. If your main point is simply to get your visual content online frequently, simply, and attractively, a No-style template is perfect. The visual content you are uploading can change without your ever needing to revise the design of your site to match it.

Finally, as in the case of Modernista! and we make money not art, No style is a way to indicate conceptual savvy. By cleverly contriving a means of *not* foregrounding your design, you effectively foreground how clever you are at contriving a means of not foregrounding your design.

● ● ●

This chapter discusses just a few No-style approaches. It would be pointless to try and exhaustively catalog all of the standard visual characteristics of No-style design, since No style has no standard visual characteristics. Instead, I've shown you a few successful conceptual approaches that might inspire further conceptual innovations.

I'm not suggesting you imitate these particular approaches whole cloth. As with conceptual art, much of the art of No-style design is in being the first one to come up with the idea. If you replicate exactly what Modernista! did, it will only seem derivative and unoriginal. But if you develop your own conceptual approaches, or even modify prior approaches in inventive ways, then you are proceeding in the proper spirit of No-style design.

The ever-present challenge with No style is to avoid having your "nothing" look like nothing simply because you were too lame to put something out there. You want to aim for purposeful, intentional nothingness. Sometimes all this takes is a subtle nod or a knowing wink.

A FRESH, EXCITING, NEW
ERA WAS BREWING OUT
OF AUTHENTIC CREATIVE
MOTIVATION, AND NOT OUT
OF AESTHETIC FORMALISM.[1]

—WOLFGANG WEINGART

03 | LATE(ST) MODERN STYLE

Although Weingart's quotation describes the beginnings of what came to be known as New Wave typography, it is equally applicable to the spirit of what I call *Late(st) Modernism*. The Late(st) Modern style is perhaps best understood as the Late(st) Modern *way*: not a fashion, but an experimental approach that seeks to push the boundaries of modernism without completely transgressing them. Of course, anyone working according to this "way" is going to create work that reflects a characteristic visual style, because every philosophical approach to design ultimately results in actual design.

The formal visual characteristics that regularly result from designing in the Late(st) Modern way aren't *all* there is to late(st) modernism, but neither are they purely incidental and inconsequential. As designers continue to push the boundaries of Late(st) Modernism, new visual characteristics will inevitably arise. Until then, the current characteristics can serve as a guide for future experimentation.

What exactly are the characteristics of the Late(st) Modern style? More than any single distinguishing visual characteristic, the style is marked by a pervasive and inherent tension between the experimental bravado of post-modern design and the structural formalism of Swiss modern design. This tension gives the style its vitality and visual interest. Late(st) Modern designers don't approach modernism slavishly, as if it were the *only* style. Postmodern design destroyed that mythology. Instead, they approach modernism as simply *another* style, but a cool, clean, intelligent style worthy of rigorous study and ripe with undisclosed possibilities.

LATE(ST) MODERN STYLE IS MARKED BY A PERVASIVE AND INHERENT TENSION BETWEEN THE EXPERIMENTAL BRAVADO OF POSTMODERN DESIGN AND THE STRUCTURAL FORMALISM OF SWISS MODERN DESIGN.

Influences

Late(st) Modern style is influenced by modernism, and by designers like Wolfgang Weingart who pushed modernism to extremes, not to destroy it, but to experimentally advance it. From this perspective, Late(st) Modernism is a continuation of modernism rather than a clean break.

Modernism

In the 1950s and 1960s, Swiss designers like Josef Müller-Brockmann and Armin Hofmann refined and purified modernist Bauhaus grid systems and sans-serif letterforms into what has been simultaneously called *Swiss modernism*, the *International Typographic style*, *high modernism*, and *late modernism*.

Fast-forward to the 1980s, and rogue designers like David Carson and Vaughan Oliver are intuitively ignoring all the tenets of modernism, abandoning grid-based layouts and standard typesetting. Their "no holds barred" design approach has been called *postmodern* or *grunge*.

Fast-forward again to the late 1990s, and a new genre of designers arise who are bored with the anarchy of postmodern design. They seek to reclaim the beauty and intention of Swiss modernism, but playfully, without all of its quasi-religious regulations and inhibitions. Their design style might be called *neomodern* or *post-postmodern*, but I call it Late(st) Modern. My term is meant to indicate the "latest," most contemporary approach to modernism. Any contemporary designer working experimentally (and not merely imitatively) in a properly modernist style is a Late(st) Modern designer.

This way, two years from now I won't have to make up a new term like Post/Pre-Retro/Futuro-Modernism, or Neo-New-Wave-Alter/Uber-Modernism. Late(st) Modernism will suffice from here on out.

Which particular modernist design masters and formal principles are most influential really depends on the individual Late(st) Modern designer. Some designers are heavily influenced by the typographic experiments of Dutch modernist Wim Crouwel. Others admire the Swiss grid systems of Josef Müller-Brockmann. Some designers revere the New York subway signage of Massimo Vignelli. Others are inspired by the minimal letterform exercises of Armin Hofmann.

Late(st) Modern designers are intimately acquainted with the work of these modernist masters. More than simply being familiar with this work, they have made it their own in some way. They have digested it. They have moved beyond the level of superficial imitation and on to the level of genuine influence. Part of this influence involves a kind of reverent irreverence. Once I have internalized and "owned" Müller-Brockmann's work, I no longer have to use grid systems exactly as he would. I am free to modify his grid systems to my own purposes. The Late(st) Modern style does not totally disregard the grid. Instead, it moves beyond slavish adherence to the grid, still stopping well shy of intuitive free play in unbounded space. It is a personal working out of modernist principles as they inform a new way of making in a new post-print medium.

Wolfgang Weingart

Wolfgang Weingart is the spiritual godfather of Late(st) Modernism. As early as the 1960s, during the peak of Swiss modernism, Weingart was one of the masters of the movement, pushing, warping, bending, and stretching its tenets to the breaking point. Unlike David Carson, whose unorthodox layouts were based on a surfer's intuition and no formal graphic design training, Weingart mastered the craft of metal typesetting à la Guttenberg. By the time he began his theoretical training under Swiss design masters Emil Ruder and Armin Hoffmann, Weingart was already immensely proficient at his craft.

Weingart took the established rules of modernism and began purposefully and rigorously breaking them—not to irreverently and anarchically destroy modernism, but to bring it to a place of greater freedom and beauty. His layouts were inspired not by a formal list of do's and don'ts, but by the desert landscapes of the Middle East. He began widely kerning letters, thus breaking up words to the point where the entire page had to be read holistically as a landscape rather than line by line. He famously developed a technique of stair-stepping words and sentences, imbuing them with a more spatial, physical, architectural quality (**Figure 3.1**). He was also interested in the textural effect of repeated letterforms, and in the tectonic properties of oversized typefaces (**Figure 3.2**).

Weingart's layouts function as typographic landscapes. They are not as free and loose as the scrawled, irregular landscapes of postmodern designers. Because Weingart never

Figure 3.1 Wolfgang Weingart's "Is this typography worth supporting or do we live on the moon?" Cover of *Typografische Monatsblätter* (1976). Film layering.

abandoned the modernist grid, his designs always maintain a formal rigor and dynamic proportion. Perhaps they are best compared to analytical cubist paintings. It is this tension between ingrained structure and energetic experimentation that gives Weingart's work its peculiar force. His layouts sometimes give off tremors, as if the tectonic plates of modernism and postmodernism were slipping past each other—grinding, snagging, and releasing alpine examples of prototypical Late(st) Modern design.

Wolfgang Weingart is the spiritual godfather of any contemporary designer wishing to return to modernism from a more experimental perspective. To return to Weingart is not to return to 1980s New Wave typography or 1960s Swiss modernism, but to return to a creative tension between modernist rules and innovative experimentation. Any contemporary web designer who is dissatisfied with the rigorous strictures of usability principles, yet unwilling to abandon formal balance for unfettered visual anarchy, is a philosophical heir of Wolfgang Weingart.

Figure 3.2 Wolfgang Weingart's "Kunstkredit Basel 1980/81" poster (1981). Film layering.

Characteristics

Although Late(st) Modernism is primarily about an overall experimental approach to modernism, rather than a formulaic set of visual tropes, such experimentation has resulted in certain visual characteristics that are worth noting. Experimenting with the modernist grid results in certain characteristic croppings, structurings, and positionings. Experimenting with sans-serif typesetting results in certain textural and architectural qualities. By examining these visual characteristics, I hope to provide a blueprint of the Late(st) Modern style.

Visible Hints of the Invisible Grid

Grid systems are most advantageously applied to books, magazines, corporate identity systems, a series of publications, a series of posters for an organization—any project in which multiple pages of content need to have a unified look. Sound familiar? Grids are particularly applicable to web design because a web site is really just a single project with a series of digital pages that need to have a unified look.

Modernist designers didn't invent the grid, but they perfected it by rigorously associating its proportions with the proportions of the typography and images they placed within it. This is why the Swiss grid is properly called the *typographic* grid. There are entire books on typographic grid systems[2], and I will only scratch the surface here, but a rudimentary understanding of the relationship between grids, typography, and photography is important in order to appreciate certain characteristic visual elements of the Late(st) Modern style.

Let's examine a basic *modular grid* layout with eight fields (**Figure 3.3**). This particular layout is for the right-facing page of a book (as evidenced by the margins surrounding the grid). Three horizontal gutters and one vertical gutter create eight fields of equal size.

In print design, font size and line leading (the space between lines of type) are particularly important in relation to the grid. The height of any individual grid field should be evenly divisible by the font size plus its line leading.

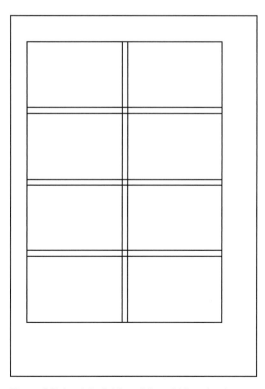

Figure 3.3 An eight-field modular grid for a book page

For example, if a single grid field is 100-points high, then I can populate that grid system with a 7-point font plus 3 points of leading (totaling 10 points). This means I will get 10 lines of text per field. Alternatively, I can populate the same grid with a 23-point font plus 2 points of leading (totaling 25 points), and get four lines of text per field. Often the horizontal gutter is sized to contain a single line of body copy plus its line leading.

This intentional mathematical relationship between type size and grid size ensures that photographs, headers, and figure captions will align precisely with any adjacent lines of body text. Every element of the design is initially harmonized to the grid so that continuity is maintained throughout the publication, regardless of the variety of its content.

Already you can see why rigorous adherence to this kind of typographic grid system is difficult for web designers: Default browser margins for paragraphs, headers, and lists won't always mathematically correspond to the font size and line leading you have chosen. To solve this problem, you have to use Cascading Style Sheets (CSS) to reset all of these HTML elements (p, ul, ol, h1, h2, h3, etc.) to mathematically correspond to your font size and leading.

For example, let's say you want to base your entire layout on a line height (font size plus leading) of 18 pixels. You use CSS to specify a body font of Verdana at 12 pixels with a line leading of 6 pixels:

```
body {
    font-family: verdana, sans-serif;
    font-size: 12px;
    line-height: 18px;
}
```

You will then have to reset your paragraph margins and your header tags to be multiples of 18 pixels. For example:

```
p {
    margin-bottom: 18px;
}
h1 {
    font-size: 24px;
    line-height: 36px;
    margin-bottom: 18px;
}
```

This at least ensures that text in one column will line up with text in another column, regardless of where the headers and paragraph breaks occur.[3]

A bigger problem with aligning web typography to a grid is that the user can always choose

GRIDS ARE PARTICULARLY APPLICABLE TO WEB DESIGN BECAUSE A WEB SITE IS REALLY JUST A SINGLE PROJECT WITH A SERIES OF DIGITAL PAGES THAT NEED TO HAVE A UNIFIED LOOK.

to drastically resize your fonts at the click of a browser button. One solution is to set your font sizes, line heights, and margins to ems (a more relative measurement than fixed pixels), so that these proportions all scale consistently when the user resizes your typography. The math is trickier than using pixels because you have to work with fractional sizes, but it's still doable.[4]

Yet another, even bigger problem is that your images still won't scale in proportion to your text. Let's assume you cropped your images to fit into a grid field 144-pixels high (18 x 8 = 144). If your line height is 18 pixels, then eight lines of text in one column will line up perfectly with a single image in an adjacent column. The baseline of the last line of text will align perfectly with the bottom edge of the adjacent image. However, once your user increases the font size, this alignment is shot.

Because the height of a modular typographic grid field is always going to be compromised whenever a user increases the font size, web designers have taken to designing layouts based on columns rather than fields, since columns

in a browser can be bottomless, expanding to accommodate the size of whatever text is placed in them.

Instead of recoding each grid system from scratch, you can use any a number of CSS *frameworks* (kind of like prefabricated templates) that have been specifically created to automate the synching of web typography and column grid layouts.[5] You can customize any of these frameworks, or create your own.

Late(st) Modern designers tend to use the more print-centric, modular typographic grid for their initial mockups and layout. Although web typography is unable to perfectly abide by the rules of the modular grid, these field-based modular grid systems yield a distinct Swiss grid aesthetic, which is not present in the more standard column grid web layouts.

CLOSELY CROPPED SQUARE AND RECTANGULAR PHOTOGRAPHS

Unlike magazine design, with its portrait layout (2-units wide by 3-units high), web design uses a landscape layout (3-units wide by 2-units

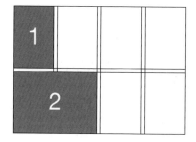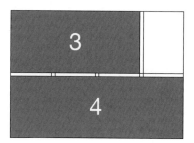

Figure 3.4 Eight possible photographic sizes of an eight-field grid

high). Let's revisit our eight-field modular grid, lose the book margins, and rotate it into a landscape format. If we want to populate this grid with photographs, we must either confine our photographs to the size of a single field, or make them evenly span multiple fields. An eight-field grid gives us eight possible photograph sizes (**Figure 3.4**). Notice that most of these sizes are rectangular. This is the result of the original rectangular layout of the entire grid, which is based on the rectangular format of a computer monitor.

Since most source photographs are rarely thin rectangles, they must be closely cropped to fit the grid. These closely cropped rectangular images are characteristic of the Late(st) Modern style (**Figure 3.5**).

Even when the source grid lines disappear and there is not enough paragraph text to reveal the underlying structure of the grid, these closely cropped photographs act as a kind of abstract, fetishistic nod to the Swiss grid era. And even when the source photographs are square, based on a nonrectangular grid,

they can still be cropped to produce this same modernist effect (**Figure 3.6**). This close cropping puts the visual primacy on the overall structure of the grid rather than on the clarity of any single image. When these images act as thumbnails linking to larger images, close-cropping has an enticing effect—teasing users just enough so that they click through without immediately giving away the entire content.

FLOATING PRODUCTS

Once your images are held securely and implicitly in place by the grid, you can remove their hard edges if you want. A photograph of a martini glass need not appear square. The glass can be photographed on a white background so that the edges of the image appear to be the silhouette of the actual martini glass. In this case, the grid provides a kind of invisible, implicit container.

This "floating" approach purposefully exceeds the goals of modernist design, which is to present the plain product as simply and objectively as possible. Ironically, to achieve this

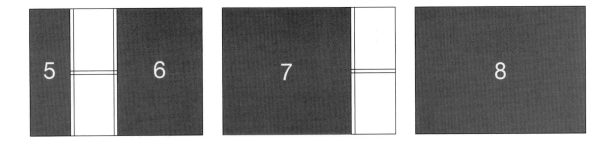

DESIGN
FOR
FREEDOM™

FRONT
SCOUTT
MUG SHOP

FREEDOM PROJECT
SHARING ARTIST
STORE

ON DISPLAY
FOCUS
CONTACT / INFO

MONDAY AUGUST 4, 2008
6:21 PM

Currently Showing

ON DISPLAY - The Dot and the Line: A Romance in Lower Mathematics is a book written and illustrated by Norton Juster, first published by Random House in 1963.

▶ View

ON DISPLAY - Ben Loiz and Friends create a mural representing team Brasil for NIKE's Joga Bonito project.

▶ View

FOCUS - Get to know Aiwei Foo and D Tan and enjoy some really wonderful things they've been making.

▶ View

ON DISPLAY - Over a period of 3 months 150 strangers were stopped on the street and asked what they where thinking about.

▶ View

July 10, 2007

Eloie

Eloie (pronounced ee-lie) was hand-crafted by Garrett Morin in an edition of 50. He stands tall at 5 inches and comes to your door in a lovingly hand-printed box. Eloie also includes two insence cones and a limited edition print.

Visit Eloie

Posted by DFF at 08:08 PM I Comments (0)

▶ **View Latest Entries**

Current Status

We've launched our product and clothing line. Checkout Ser-vice® because it's good.

—

We're strong supporters of the planet and our environment. We hope that the companies and the people who have the ability to change our current energy sources will step up and move our cultures toward a more earth friendly way of life.

More information is available here: exxposeexxon.com

This site includes information on how you can assist in making a change.

—

Enjoyable Viewing

4.6.07

aes
madethought
blog.pentagram
famewhore
emilkozak

trevor-jackson
rgbstudio
bantjes
stevenharrington
everyoneforever

▶ View Archive

Hosting

DESIGNFORFREEDOM would like to thank Media Temple for providing solid hosting serivices. We love Bandwidth.

(mt) mediatemple

DESIGNFORFREEDOM™
©2006 All Rights Reserved Contact - Mailing List

Figure 3.5 designforfreedom.com

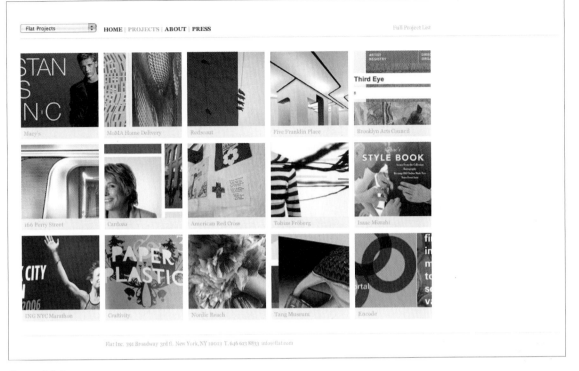

Figure 3.6 flat.com

purely objective perspective, modernist designers had to escape reality and enter a detached, free-floating, quasi-neutral space of ideals and pure forms.

The product photographs framed and taken from this detached perspective wound up being a highly successful marketing tool. Consumers weren't buying these products because they were neutrally and objectively displayed, but because they promised an entrance into this ideal, floating, perfectly gridded and harmonized realm—a fantasy modernist heaven.

Target is a great example of this approach. Its in-store displays and the product catalogs on target.com take this tradition of floating design to intentional extremes. The products are presented alone on a neutral background, totally abstracted from any specific kitchen, backyard, or natural environment. The clothing is worn by models who float effortlessly in negative space, without any ground plane or real-world background. These advertisements are selling the implicit promise of ideal disembodiment. They are selling a ticket to transcend the messy world in which we actually live, and enter a cleaner, more antiseptic one.

helmutlang.com is a gorgeous example of gridded, floating photographs of models who look almost angelic, or ghostly, depending on your interpretation (**Figure 3.7**). Each thumbnail invites a click, if only to give these models some substance and keep them from disappearing altogether into waifish oblivion. What remains in the visitor's mind is not the models or even the garments, but the ideal of a weightless paradise laid out on a perfect grid.

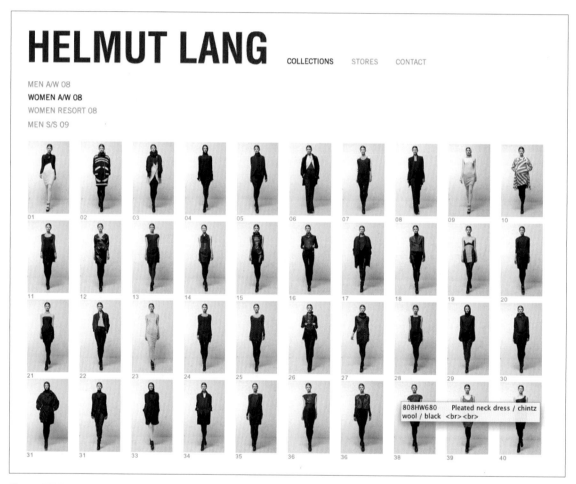

Figure 3.7 helmutlang.com

Figure 3.8 designforfreedom.com

ABSTRACT RESIDUAL GRID MARKS

Just because your layout is based on a grid doesn't mean that the structure of your grid will automatically be apparent once you hide your grid guidelines. Your grid's structure is only made visible by the content you align to it. The more sparsely and irregularly you populate your grid with content, the less visible your underlying grid structure will be. Since part of the abstract fetishism of Late(st) Modernism is to make the grid structure apparent, a lack of grid-revealing content can be supplemented by the addition of residual grid markings. The idea is not to make the entire grid visible (à la graph paper), but to more subtly reveal purposefully placed ticks, edges, plusses, crosshatchings, lines, bars, and other elements at carefully chosen locations and increments.

Design For Freedom's homepage has a thin, dark gray, horizontal line at the very top of the page, interrupted by subtle, light gray vertical ticks which indicate the underlying structure of the site's grid system (**Figure 3.8**). These light gray ticks are subtly echoed at the bottom of the header area by barely perceptible, slightly darker, horizontal gray ticks. The thin, dark gray line is repeated as a short vertical tick in the top right hand corner of each content box, anchoring each box to the grid and offsetting the dark gray horizontal header bar in the left corner of each box.

These structural markings act like subconscious hints—traces of the grid, seductive hide-and-seek teases that suggest the grid's form without blatantly revealing its full structure. Such residual grid marks invite the viewer to mentally complete the grid, even if this involvement is only subconscious. These grid marks suggest the transcendent structural order of a container without the embodied clunkiness of the actual container.

Geotectonic Typography

Classic modernism has always implicitly (and sometimes overtly) embraced the idea of "architectonic typography," or typography that has been influenced by the principles and forms of architecture. All three directors of the Bauhaus—Walter Gropius, Hannes Meyer, and Ludwig Mies van der Rohe—were architects. To understand the principles of geotectonic typography, it is useful to have an understanding of architectonic typography.

The theory behind architectonic typography is that architecture is the ultimate manifestation of design, since it encompasses the very space in which one lives and works. The idea is that if you can master architecture, then you can also master furniture design, graphic design, and typeface design. According to this way of thinking, design ranges from the macrocosmic (architecture) to the microcosmic (typography). So ideally, the typography in your coffee table book harmonizes with the grid system of the book itself, which harmonizes with the proportions of the coffee table, the room, the house, the city, and, ultimately, your tightly integrated modernist universe. No wonder there was a postmodern revolt!

Wolfgang Weingart's typography extends beyond the merely architectonic and approaches the geotectonic. Rather than base his typographic experiments solely on man-made modernist architectural principles, Weingart based his experiments on the desert landscapes and ancient architectural ruins of the Middle East. Sometimes his sentences dance and stair-step like abstract Arabic ornamentation. Other times his blocks of text tower as epic, geological structures—more like earthworks than buildings. Weingart's desert landscape approach to typography is particularly applicable to the horizontal landscape format of web design.

A TYPEFACE IS AS MUCH ABOUT THE NEGATIVE SPACE SURROUNDING AND WITHIN THE LETTERFORM AS IT IS ABOUT THE POSITIVE SPACE OF THE PRINTED LETTERFORM.

TEXT AS TEXTURE

Modernist designers worked with a limited number of (usually) sans-serif faces. It was kind of a badge of honor to see how much design mileage you could get out of the fewest typefaces possible. Weingart used to limit himself to four faces, preferring Akzident Grotesque (the precursor to Helvetica) because it had a brokenness that gave it character.[6] The challenge became how to push the rigid boundaries of modernist typography while still using a limited number of sans-serif faces. Weingart couldn't rely on the shortcut use of "expressive" grunge typefaces to push these boundaries, because grunge faces hadn't been invented yet. He instead relied on his own creative typesetting to make the more neutral, geometric sans-serif faces arresting and vivid.

Classic modernist typography was meant first and foremost to be legible, neutral, and subservient to the content of the text. Yet modernist sans-serif typefaces still have their own formal characteristics. A typeface is as much about the negative space surrounding and within the letterform as it is about the positive space of the printed letterform.

Each typeface has a different color when set as paragraphs on a page. A thin sans-serif face will create a lighter color than a thick blackletter face. This is not because the thin face is printed in gray ink, but because a full page of text set with a thin face is holistically perceived as lighter, since there is a greater ratio of negative white space to positive black space. Print typographers compensate for these differences in type color by increasing or decreasing leading (the vertical space between lines) and kerning (the horizontal space between letters). The goal of modernist design is an even gray color that doesn't distract from the content of the text.

The fact that each typeface (even supposedly neutral sans-serif faces like Helvetica) has its own characteristic color suggests a way to push and break modernist typesetting. By repeating the same words on a page, by setting words consecutively with minimal kerning and leading, letterforms begin to assume their own abstract texture apart from what they denotatively say. Typography lumped or massed together can assume a kind of colossal structure and weight.

Late(st) Modern web designers transform ordinary link lists into abstract typesetting experiments. For example, at the online portfolio site of photographer Christine Woditschka, each text link is grossly oversized, separated only by double vertical hash marks that are the same color as the links themselves (**Figure 3.9**).

Since the text is set flush left and ragged right, the large typography size ensures that the ragged-right edge will contain dramatic white space gaps that contrast asymmetrically with the flush-left edge.

When you roll over the links, the page reveals more form and texture by taking advantage of the CSS background-color property for link rollovers (**Figure 3.10**). Each rollover reveals a different, solidly shaped gray form in place of the text for that link. Since the links are large and span multiple lines, the gray forms are not simply rectangular, but form a variety of stair-step patterns. This is what I call the

christine woditschka
cv
kontakt
johannisthal berlin 2007-1 II johannisthal
berlin 2007-2 II johannisthal berlin 2007-3 II
johannisthal berlin 2007-4 II johannisthal
berlin 2007 garten-1 II johannisthal berlin 2007
garten-2 II norra vinstorp 2007-1 II norra
vinstorp 2007-2 II norra vinstorp 2007-3 II
norra vinstorp 2007-4 II schweizer viertel
berlin 2006-1 II schweizer viertel berlin 2006-2
II plattenbau berlin 2006-1 II plattenbau berlin
2006-2 II plattenbau berlin 2006-3 II plattenbau
berlin 2006-4 II plattenbau eisenhuettenstadt
2006-1 II plattenbau eisenhuettenstadt 2006-2
II plattenbau eisenhuettenstadt 2006-3 II
plattenbau eisenhuettenstadt 2006-4 II
siedlung annahoeh berlin 2006 1 II siedlung
annahoeh berlin 2006 2 II siedlung annahoeh
berlin 2006 3 II siedlung annahoeh berlin 2006
4 II siedlung neulindenberg brandenburg 2006
nachtfahrt 1 II siedlung neulindenberg
brandenburg 2006 nachtfahrt 2 II siedlung
neulindenberg brandenburg 2006 nachtfahrt 3
II siedlung neulindenberg brandenburg 2006
nachtfahrt 4 II buerogebaeude berlin 2005
flashlight-1 II buerogebaeude berlin 2005
flashlight-2 II buerogebaeude berlin 2005
flashlight-3 II buerogebaeude berlin 2005
flashlight-4 II

Figure 3.9 christinewoditschka.com

plattenbau eisenhuettenstadt 2006-4 II
siedlung annahoeh berlin 2006 1 II siedlung
annahoeh berlin 2006 2 II siedlung annahoeh
berlin 2006 3 II siedlung annahoeh berlin 2006
4 II siedlung neulindenberg brandenburg 2006
nachtfahrt 1 II siedlung neulindenberg
brandenburg 2006 nachtfahrt 2 II

II siedlung neulindenberg brandenburg 2006
nachtfahrt 4 II buerogebaeude berlin 2005
flashlight-1 II buerogebaeude berlin 2005
flashlight-2 II buerogebaeude berlin 2005
flashlight-3 II buerogebaeude berlin 2005
flashlight-4 II

Figure 3.10 christinewoditschka.com rollover states

plattenbau eisenhuettenstadt 2006-4 II
siedlung annahoeh berlin 2006 1 II siedlung
annahoeh berlin 2006 2 II siedlung annahoeh
berlin 2006 3 II siedlung annahoeh berlin 2006
4 II

II siedlung neulindenberg
brandenburg 2006 nachtfahrt 2 II siedlung
neulindenberg brandenburg 2006 nachtfahrt 3
II siedlung neulindenberg brandenburg 2006
nachtfahrt 4 II buerogebaeude berlin 2005
flashlight-1 II buerogebaeude berlin 2005
flashlight-2 II buerogebaeude berlin 2005
flashlight-3 II buerogebaeude berlin 2005
flashlight-4 II

Weingart Rollover effect. On the web, these stair-step patterns of inversed text and background don't need to remain visible all the time; they can hide until a rollover reveals them.

The portfolio site for installation artist Katharina Grosse employs a similar textured link list, except this time the link text is smaller, multicolored (befitting the artist's multicolored work), and not separated by punctuation at all (**Figure 3.11**).

Since Grosse's artworks are untitled, each link text simply lists the media in which the piece was made. For example, if Grosse has fifteen pieces that she created using acrylic on a wall, then the site displays fifteen links that say "acrylic on wall." The entire link list becomes a kind of run-on concrete poem about Grosse's particular approach to mixed media.

Rolling over any single link surrounds it with a black box, pulling it out of the run-on sentence and focusing attention on the specific media used in that particular work. Once links are visited, a permanent black box surrounds those links, which keeps you from visiting the same "acrylic on wall" link twice (**Figure 3.12**).

In addition to the text links, there is a chronological list of "year" links at the top of the page. Once you've viewed a piece of work created during one of those years, that year link also gets the black-box treatment. Surfing the site becomes a kind of enticing game. You want to see all the pieces in order to transform the entire colorful link list into white text on black boxes.

TEXT AS STRUCTURE

Another way to get interesting visual mileage with a limited typeface palette is by making your text large and monumental. For any typography to seem large, it must be set next to small typography. This relative contrast in sizes can make the large text seem dramatically monumental in context.

Large sans-serif type, set flush left and ragged right, can have an almost startling effect. When set as a subtle, only slightly larger header in a classic modernist layout, this typographic treatment might be called *architectonic*. But when the same header type is set much larger for an intentionally dramatic effect, this is an example of geotectonic typography.

Let's take a look at three examples that run the gamut from only slightly larger than classic modernist header type to off-the-chain, enormous header type.

The portfolio site for the design firm Kind Company begins with a two-sentence welcome and explanation: "hello. kind company designs web sites, printed materials + identities" (**Figure 3.13**). These words are set in lowercase sans serif, with only a slight bold on the name of the company to highlight it. The typeface itself is subtle, but it is not set subtly. It is by far the largest text on the page (apart from the fragments of text in the closely cropped thumbnail images), dwarfing the nearby linking text of the site's navigation menu. The contrast of understated typeface and overstated type size creates an arresting tension—kind of like whispering loudly.

Grosse Info Contact Work:

0000 0000 0000 1995 1995 1995 1996 1996 1998 1998 1998 1998 1998 1999 1999 1999 1999 1999 1999 2000 2000 2000 2000 2001 2001 2001 2001 2001 2001 2001 2001 200
2002 2002 2002 2002 **2002** 2002 2002 2002 2002 2002 2003 2003 2003 2003 2003 2003 2003 2003 2003 2003 2003 2003 2003 2003 2004 2004 2004 2004 2004 2004 200
2004 2005 2005 2005 2005 2005 2005 2006 2006 2006 2006 2006 2006 2006 2006 2006 2006 2006 2006 2007 2007 2007 2007 2007 2007 2007 2007 2008 200
acrylic on acrylic plaster on styrofoam acrylic on acrylic plaster on styrofoam acrylic on acrylic plaster on styrofoam acrylic on balloons, soil, walls, floor acrylic on
billboard acrylic on canvas acrylic on canvas acrylic on canvas acrylic on canvas acrylic on canvas acrylic on canvas acrylic on canvas acrylic on canvas acrylic on canvas
acrylic on canvas acrylic on canvas acrylic on canvas acrylic on canvas acrylic on canvas acrylic on canvas acrylic on canvas acrylic on canvas acrylic on canvas acrylic on
canvas acrylic on canvas acrylic on canvas, walls and ceiling acrylic on concrete flooor, clothes, books, and eggs acrylic on floor and canvas acrylic on floor and wall acryli
on glass, metal and brick Acrylic on paper, floor and wall acrylic on pvc carpeting, clothes, books, and eggs acrylic on soil, floor, steel container and tin shelves acrylic on
styrofoam on polyurethane on wood acrylic on wall acrylic on wall acrylic on wall acrylic on wall acrylic on wall acrylic on wall acrylic on wall acrylic on wall acrylic on wa
acrylic on wall acrylic on wall acrylic on wall acrylic on wall acrylic on wall acrylic on wall acrylic on wall acrylic on wall acrylic on wall acrylic on wall and
book shelf acrylic on wall and canvas acrylic on wall and foam acrylic on wall and various objects acrylic on wall, bookshelf and canvases acrylic on wall, ceiling, soil, late
balloons and canvases acrylic on wall, floor and latex balloons acrylic on wall, floor and rock acrylic on wall, floor and styrofoam on polyurethane on wood acrylic on wall,
floor and table tops acrylic on wall, floor and various elements acrylic on wall, floor, canvas and soil acrylic on wall, floor, ceiling, bed, canvas, books and clot acrylic on
wall, floor, clothes, plywood and stones acrylic on wall, floor, futon, books, clothes and canvas acrylic on wall, floor, glas, styrofoam and soil acrylic on wall, floor, glas,
styrofoam and soil acrylic on wall, floor, rock and various objects acrylic on wall, floor, soil and 2 canvases acrylic on wall, floor, soil and canvas acrylic on wall, floor, so
styrofoam boards and canvas acrylic on wall, pvc carpeting and canvas acrylic on wall, PVC carpeting, canvas and latex balloons acrylic on wall, styrofoam boards and soil
acrylic on walls, floor and canvases acrylic/soil on canvas Amsterdam Art Unlimited/Art Basel Artium de Álava Atomimage Atoms outside Eggs Auckland
Auckland Barbara Gross Galerie Basel Bergen Berlin Berlin Berlin Berlinische Galerie Bern Biennale of Sydney, Art Gallery of New South Wales Birmingham Bochum Bonn
Bozen Brisbane CASO Cheese Gone Bad Chicago Chicago Chinati Foundation Christopher Grimes Gallery Cincinnati Cincy Clermont-Ferrand Clermont-Ferrand Contemporary
Arts Center Contemporary Arts Museum Houston Copenhagen De Appel dimensions variable Double Floor Painting Dusseldorf Dusseldorf Düsseldorf Essen exterior exterior
exterior exterior Faux Rocks Faux Rocks Flowershow FRAC Auvergne FRAC Auvergne Frankfurt Frankfurter Kunstverein Friedrich Petzel Gallery Galeria Filomena Soares
Galeria Helga de Alvear Galerie Conrads Galerie Mark Müller Galerie nächst St. Stephan Gow Langsford Gallery Haifa Haifa Museum of Art Hamburg Helsinki Houston If
Music No Good I No Dance Ikon Gallery Infinite Logic Conference installation interior interior interior interior interior interior interior interior interior
interior interior interior interior interior interior interior interior Interior Interior Jüchen Karlsruhe Kiasma - Museum of Contemporary Art kum kum Kunsthall
Bergen Kunsthalle Bern Kunsthalle Düsseldorf and Kunstverein für die Rheinlande und Westfalen Kunsthallen Brandts Klædefabrik Kunstmuseum Bonn Kunstverein Ruhr
Leeuwarden Lelystad Lisbon London Los Angeles Los Angeles Madrid Magasin 3 Stockholm Konsthall Marfa Meyer Riegger Galerie Milan Milan mineral silicate paint on wal
Mori Art Museum Munich Museion Museu de Arte Contemporânea de Serralves Museu de Arte Contemporânea de Serralves Museum Bochum Nationalgalerie im Hamburger
Bahnhof Neue Nationalgalerie New York New York Nürnberg o.T. Odense oil on canvas oil on canvas oil on canvas oil on canvas oil on canvas oil-acrylic on wall oil-acrylic
on canvas Osaka PAC painting paintings paintings paintings paintings paintings paintings paintings paintings paintings paintings paintings paintings paintings paintings
paintings paintings paintings paintings paintings paintings Palais de Tokyo Paris Pearson International Airport Picture Park Pigmentos Para Plantas y Globos Porto Porto
Queensland Art Gallery Reykjavik Richmond SAFN Schloß Dyck Siemens SKROW NO REPAP Solvent Space Something Leadlight Stockholm Sydney Taipei Taipei Fine Arts
Museum Taxi und Tour Telekomgebäude The Child Care and Protection Agency The Drawing Center The Factory for Art and Design The Flowershow The Poise of the Head
und die anderen folgen The Renaissance Society The Suburban This is Not Dogshit This Is Not My Cat tiles/ Tokyo Toronto Town And Country UCLA Hammer Museum Union
untitled untitled untitled untitled untitled untitled untitled untitled untitled untitled untitled untitled untitled untitled untitled untitled untitled untitled
Untitled Untitled Untitled Untitled Untitled Untitled Viafarini Vitoria-Gasteiz Wesel Y8 International Sivananda Yoga-Center Zürich

Figure 3.11 katharinagrosse.com

Grosse Info Contact Work:

0000 0000 0000 1995 1995 1995 1996 1996 1998 1998 1998 1998 1998 1999 1999 1999 1999 1999 1999 2000 2000 2000 2000 2001 2001 2001 2001 2001 2001 2001 2001 2002
2002 2002 2002 2002 2002 2002 2002 2002 2002 2002 2003 2003 2003 2003 2003 2003 2003 2003 2003 2003 2003 2003 2003 2003 2004 2004 2004 2004 2004 2004 2004
2004 2005 2005 2005 2005 2005 2005 2006 2006 2006 2006 2006 2006 2006 2006 2006 2006 2006 2006 2007 2007 2007 2007 2007 2007 2007 2007 2008 2008
acrylic on acrylic plaster on styrofoam acrylic on acrylic plaster on styrofoam acrylic on acrylic plaster on styrofoam acrylic on balloons, soil, walls, floor acrylic on
billboard acrylic on canvas acrylic on canvas acrylic on canvas acrylic on canvas acrylic on canvas acrylic on canvas acrylic on canvas acrylic on canvas acrylic on canvas
acrylic on canvas acrylic on canvas acrylic on canvas acrylic on canvas acrylic on canvas acrylic on canvas acrylic on canvas acrylic on canvas acrylic on canvas acrylic on
canvas acrylic on canvas acrylic on canvas, walls and ceiling acrylic on concrete flooor, clothes, books, and eggs acrylic on floor and canvas acrylic on floor and wall acrylic
on glass, metal and brick Acrylic on paper, floor and wall acrylic on pvc carpeting, clothes, bed, walls and acrylic on soil, floor, steel container and tin shelves acrylic on
styrofoam on polyurethane on wood acrylic on wall acrylic on wall acrylic on wall acrylic on wall acrylic on wall acrylic on wall acrylic on wall acrylic on wall acrylic on wall
wall acrylic on wall acrylic on wall acrylic on wall acrylic on wall acrylic on wall acrylic on wall acrylic on wall acrylic on wall acrylic on wall acrylic on wall
and book shelf acrylic on wall and canvas acrylic on wall and foam acrylic on wall and various objects acrylic on wall, bookshelf and canvases acrylic on wall, ceiling, soil,
latex balloons and canvases acrylic on wall, floor and latex balloons acrylic on wall, floor and rock acrylic on wall, floor and styrofoam on polyurethane on wood acrylic on
wall, floor and table tops acrylic on wall, floor and various elements acrylic on wall, floor, canvas and soil acrylic on wall, floor, ceiling, bed, canvas, books and clot acrylic
on wall, floor, clothes, plywood and stones acrylic on wall, floor, futon, books, clothes and canvas acrylic on wall, floor, glas, styrofoam and soil acrylic on wall, floor, glas,
styrofoam and soil acrylic on wall, floor, rock and various objects acrylic on wall, floor, soil and 2 canvases acrylic on wall, floor, soil and canvas acrylic on wall, floor, soil,
styrofoam boards and canvas acrylic on wall, pvc carpeting and canvas acrylic on wall, PVC carpeting, canvas and latex balloons acrylic on wall, styrofoam boards and soil
acrylic on walls, floor and canvases acrylic on wood acrylic/soil on canvas Amsterdam Art Unlimited/Art Basel Artium de Álava Atomimage Atoms outside Eggs Auckland
Auckland Barbara Gross Galerie Basel Bergen Berlin Berlin Berlin Berlinische Galerie Bern Biennale of Sydney, Art Gallery of New South Wales Birmingham Bochum Bonn
Bozen Brisbane CASO Cheese Gone Bad Chicago Chicago Chinati Foundation Christopher Grimes Gallery Cincinnati Cincy Clermont-Ferrand Clermont-Ferrand Contemporary
Arts Center Contemporary Arts Museum Houston Copenhagen De Appel dimensions variable Double Floor Painting Dusseldorf Dusseldorf Düsseldorf Essen exterior exterior
exterior exterior Faux Rocks Faux Rocks Flowershow FRAC Auvergne FRAC Auvergne Frankfurt Frankfurter Kunstverein Friedrich Petzel Gallery Galeria Filomena Soares
Galeria Helga de Alvear Galerie Conrads Galerie Mark Müller Galerie nächst St. Stephan Gow Langsford Gallery Haifa Haifa Museum of Art Hamburg Helsinki Houston If
Music No Good I No Dance Ikon Gallery Infinite Logic Conference installation interior interior interior interior interior interior interior interior interior
interior Interior interior Interior interior interior interior interior interior interior Interior Interior Jüchen Karlsruhe Kiasma - Museum of Contemporary Art kum kum Kunsthall
Bergen Kunsthalle Bern Kunsthalle Düsseldorf and Kunstverein für die Rheinlande und Westfalen Kunsthallen Brandts Klædefabrik Kunstmuseum Bonn Kunstverein Ruhr
Leeuwarden Lelystad Lisbon London Los Angeles Los Angeles Madrid Magasin 3 Stockholm Konsthall Marfa Meyer Riegger Galerie Milan Milan mineral silicate paint on wall
Mori Art Museum Munich Museion Museu de Arte Contemporânea de Serralves Museu de Arte Contemporânea de Serralves Museum Bochum Nationalgalerie im Hamburger
Bahnhof Neue Nationalgalerie New York New York Nürnberg o.T. Odense oil on canvas oil on canvas oil on canvas oil on canvas oil on canvas oil-acrylic on wall oil-acrylics
on canvas Osaka PAC painting paintings paintings paintings paintings paintings paintings paintings paintings paintings paintings paintings paintings paintings paintings
paintings paintings paintings paintings paintings Palais de Tokyo Paris Pearson International Airport Picture Park Pigmentos Para Plantas y Globos Porto Porto
Queensland Art Gallery Reykjavik Richmond SAFN Schloß Dyck Siemens SKROW NO REPAP Solvent Space Something Leadlight Stockholm Sydney Taipei Taipei Fine Arts
Museum Taxi und Tour Telekomgebäude The Child Care and Protection Agency The Drawing Center The Factory for Art and Design The Flowershow The Poise of the Head
und die anderen folgen The Renaissance Society The Suburban This is Not Dogshit This Is Not My Cat tiles/ Tokyo Toronto Town And Country UCLA Hammer Museum Union
untitled untitled untitled untitled untitled untitled untitled untitled untitled untitled untitled untitled untitled untitled untitled
Untitled Untitled Untitled Untitled Untitled Untitled Viafarini Vitoria-Gasteiz Wesel Y8 International Sivananda Yoga-Center Zürich

Figure 3.12 katharinagrosse.com visited link states

Figure 3.13 kindcompany.com

On this portfolio site, there is not a lot of body copy, so the header mostly needs to be scaled in proportion to the thumbnail images. The header text itself is not colossal, but the space in the grid surrounding the header text is. The top 250 pixels of the page are set aside for nothing but the header text and its surrounding white space.

The design challenge for this site was how to keep the header from being overwhelmed by the large, colorful, visually complex portfolio thumbnails without making it into some giant, screaming edifice. Kind Company achieves the solution via contextual typography. The face itself is subtle and the sentences are playful, so the screaming problem is solved. And since the header is surrounded by abundant negative space and placed next to very tiny navigation type, it is also able to hold its own visually with the thumbnail images.

The portfolio site for the marketing firm Poccuo also features a large welcome sentence (**Figure 3.14**). The sentence is drawn from a regularly updated database of random phrases that change when you revisit the site. The phrases playfully describe the daily activity of the four employees of the firm.

The typography of the Poccuo sentence is heavier than the Kind Company header type, yet the Poccuo sentence seems slightly less dramatic. Why? For one reason, it is placed next to other type of similar size (the Poccuo logo). So the jump between its size and the next largest type size nearby is less drastic. For another reason, although the sentence is also offset by a lot of surrounding white space for emphasis, it doesn't appear at the very top of the page. The sentence is subordinate to the logo and navigation bar. This subordination makes sense, because the sentence is merely a friendly addition to the site, and not meant to serve as a logo or mission statement like the Kind Company welcome header.

The face used for the Poccuo sentence is serif (40-pixel Georgia). A hardcore modernist might argue that a serif face makes the sentence more elitist, more antique, and less populist (although Georgia itself wasn't created until 1993). A Late(st) Modern designer knows that serif faces can actually make a sentence less sterile, more old-fashioned, plain-spoken, and personably conversational. The use of blue also makes the sentence seem informal and playful. And of course the copy itself is playful.

Poccuo applies a modern layout treatment to a premodern typeface (a very postmodern thing to do). The mixture of serif and sans-serif faces in this modernist layout creates a clever, purposeful tension. Props to Poccuo for using Georgia set large. Web designers don't have that many browser-safe HTML typefaces to choose from[7], so creative typesetting (increasing size,

A LATE(ST) MODERN DESIGNER KNOWS THAT SERIF FACES CAN ACTUALLY MAKE A SENTENCE LESS STERILE, MORE OLD-FASHIONED, PLAIN-SPOKEN, AND PERSONABLY CONVERSATIONAL.

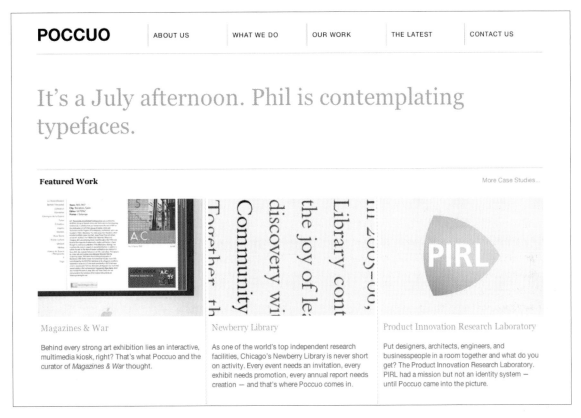

Figure 3.14 poccuo.com

decreasing letter-spacing, increasing surrounding negative space, and so on) is required to get the most mileage and variation out of them.

Finally, the welcome page of photographer Pep Karsten delivers one possible extreme of geotectonic typography (**Figure 3.15**).

This page doesn't contain any photographic thumbnails, so there is nothing to visually compete with the three massive lines of bold,

all-uppercase, sans-serif text. The smaller, all-uppercase lines of text directly below make the large text seem even larger by contrast. The letters are kerned tightly, and there is almost no leading. The result is a mountainous bulk of massive letterforms—geotectonic typography.

The three lines of text are actually a single .gif image that gets swapped out on the rollover for another .gif with two new lines of

Figure 3.15 pepkarsten.com

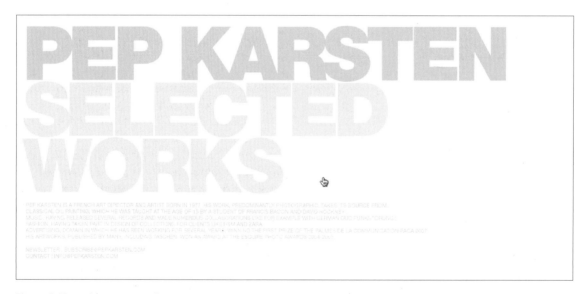

Figure 3.16 pepkarsten.com rollover state

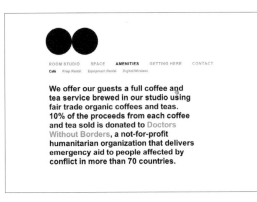

Figure 3.17 roomstudio.net

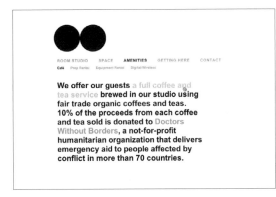

Figure 3.18 roomstudio.net rollover state

Figure 3.19 roomstudio.net active link state

text (**Figure 3.16**). The rollover effect further enhances the raggedness of the right edge. As you roll over the image, it feels more like boulders shifting than mere letterforms toggling—the tectonic grinding of typographic granite.

Minimal Palettes

In addition to grid systems and typography, many Late(st) Modern designers use extremely minimal color palettes as a way of celebrating and exaggerating the minimalist restraint of modernism. In extreme cases, only black typography on white background is used. Links are simply indicated by black underlines. In other cases, a grayscale palette is used.

The web site for Room Studio incorporates a grayscale palette (**Figure 3.17**). Links are indicated with gray text, and rolling over them turns them into black text (**Figure 3.18**). A wild-card yellow appears startlingly and briefly during the active link state, the split second that the mouse button is pressed down when the link is clicked (**Figure 3.19**).

Late(st) Modern designers consider it a challenge to achieve innovative visual effects with a limited set of typefaces and a limited number of colors. As with much graphic design, limitations can actually be advantages in disguise. They require a higher degree of ingenuity, and often lead to unique and unforeseen results. In the next chapter, we'll see the addition of vibrant color to the Late(st) Modern style, transforming it into the paradoxically titled *Psychedelic Minimalist* style. But we're not there yet.

Background Killer: Grayscale Diagonals and Dots

The classic and obvious background killer approach for the Late(st) Modern style is negative white space. However, if you're feeling a bit more adventurous, another approach is to use tiling, diagonal, grayscale lines, or tiling, evenly spaced, grayscale dots. Using dots and dashes in graphic design is a basic means of achieving texture without overwhelming the rest of your layout.

The web site deform-group.com uses very subtle 7-pixel-wide gray stripes, alternated with larger 14-pixel-wide white stripes, all set at a 45-degree angle, to kill the extra space to the right of the content area on screen resolutions over 1000-pixels wide (**Figure 3.20**). The entire pattern is saved as a 270-by-150-pixel-high .gif, and then used as the tiling background of the page.

At serviceisgood.com, dots are used to add texture to the product area, and the extra background space is actually killed by the company logotype and motto tiled at a 20-degree angle (**Figure 3.21**).

Finally, at the Nasher Museum of Art site, gray diagonals are used more sparingly as content fillers within the grid to indicate its implicit structure, as described in the "Abstract residual grid marks" section (**Figure 3.22**).

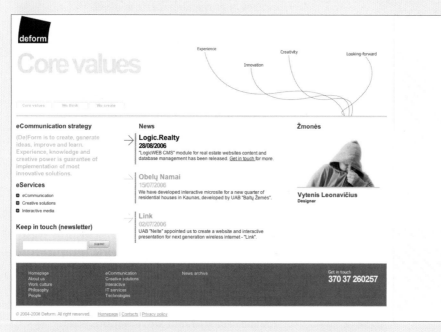

Figure 3.20 deform-group.com

Figure 3.21 serviceisgood.com

Figure 3.22 nasher.duke.edu

Uses

Because of its strong grid structure, the Late(st) Modern style is useful for catalog sites (like Helmut Lang), portfolio sites (like Kind Company and Poccuo), or any site with a lot of photographic content that needs to be cleanly featured. Its minimal color palette puts the focus on the images themselves; its close-cropping adds visual interest to the thumbnails; and its ability to cleanly showcase floating silhouetted products adds an element of weightless, ideal perfection to even the most mundane products.

Late(st) Modern style is particularly appropriate for products usually associated with modernism: European automobiles, modern furniture, and modern architecture. Any site meant to be explicitly associated with historical modernism is a candidate for this style. As with any style, the tenets of Late(st) Modernism can be applied at whatever degree best suits the project. Some sites will want to look more experimental, contemporary, and post-postmodern (like katharinagrosse.com). Other sites will simply want to look clean and modern, with only a modicum of Weingartian playfulness (like roomstudio.net).

● ● ●

According to sociologist Bruno Latour, modernism always leads to the proliferation of hybrids. This is because modernism presumes false dichotomies (like nature/culture), and then proceeds to create as if these dichotomies were actually true. This leads to the development of hybrid nature-culture forms that spawn while no one is looking. The same thing happens with modernist design. When ornamentation and subjective personal expression are divorced from utility and function, what proliferates is a hybrid style in which subjective expression plays freely using the very building blocks of rigorous formalism. Such hybridness, far from being antithetical to modernism, is actually inherent to it. It should come as no surprise that some of the most radically inventive graphic designers of the 21st Century list Helvetica as their favorite typeface. Modernism is dead. Long live modernism!

OUR LITTLE LIVES GET
COMPLICATED

IT'S A SIMPLE THING

SIMPLE AS A FLOWER

AND THAT'S A
COMPLICATED THING

—LOVE AND ROCKETS

04 | *PSYCHEDELIC MINIMALIST STYLE*

The Psychedelic Minimalist style is a schizophrenic combination of two seemingly contradictory approaches. Its layout and typography are very simple, basic, and minimal, but its color and ornamentation are wild, bright, florescent, and psychedelic. The Psychedelic Minimalist style is kind of like the Late(st) Modern style on LSD. Grayscale palettes are replaced by bright screen colors—colors that only exist in RGB light space and are very difficult to replicate in CMYK print space.

This conflict between understated layout structures and unapologetically bright colors gives Psychedelic Minimalism its playful tension. Rather than pushing every element of site design toward ornate psychedelic extremes, the Psychedelic Minimalist style intentionally straddles the fence between minimalism and psychedelia, achieving surprisingly fresh, purposefully paradoxical results.

Influences

The influences of Psychedelic Minimalism come from two completely different, oppositional eras. It is partially influenced by 1920s European modernism, but its colors are influenced by 1960s California psychedelic art, which was a reaction against modernism.

1960s Psychedelic Color Schemes

Psychedelic poster art of the late 1960s is famous for its barely legible art nouveau-inspired typography, its use of organic forms, and its vibrant colors. Psychedelic Minimalism retains the vibrant colors and discards everything else. Psychedelic minimalists are more influenced by the muted, iridescent, pastel color schemes of pop artist Peter Max than by the intense, intrusive, seizure-inducing color schemes of psychedelic illustrator Victor Moscoso. In this sense, the colors of Psychedelic Minimalism might be considered *psychedelic lite*—a happy, neon rainbow trip rather than a heavy, hardcore, mind-eroding one.

Because the colors of Psychedelic Minimalist style are used sparingly, they don't often have the opportunity to intensely vibrate in contrast to one another, which is just fine. These color combinations don't need to be optically intense in order to seem intense. Set in the context of a minimal layout scheme, even a slightly vibrant hue screams brightly.

The "Less Is More" Minimalist Mantra

Modernist architect and Bauhaus director Ludwig Mies van der Rohe famously adopted the motto "Less is more." He sought to use the minimum of formal elements necessary to achieve his required goals. This approach characterizes minimalism. There is no wasted effort, no ornamentation, no fluff. Psychedelic minimalists adopt the Less Is More mantra and apply it to everything but color and texture. Layout schemes are direct and sparse. Right angles dominate. There is a lack of flowing, organic, ornamental line. Typography is standard and straightforward.

The addition of vibrant colors to this extremely reserved design approach is an intentionally playful move. Curiously, psychedelic colors in a minimalist environment don't come across as anarchic or even accidental. Because everything else is so purposefully structured, the vibrant colors themselves look purposeful and contained. The minimalism tames the psychedelia.

CURIOUSLY, PSYCHEDELIC COLORS IN A MINIMALIST ENVIRONMENT DON'T COME ACROSS AS ANARCHIC OR EVEN ACCIDENTAL.

Characteristics

The minimalist layouts of the Psychedelic Minimalist style are a given. They are achieved by conservatively applying modernist grid systems (see Chapter 3 for a more detailed discussion of grid systems). Here I will focus on the psychedelic characteristics of Psychedelic Minimalism: color and its application.

Psychedelic Minimalist color schemes include bright, unrestrained colors, but only a few per palette. It's not a kaleidoscopic freak-fest of dozens of unrelated colors. The colors in each palette are visually related to each other. The saturation and value of each palette are very similar, with only the actual hues differing. One site might contain four related neon colors; another might contain six related pastel colors.

Many of the screenshots in this chapter don't really do justice to the pure, electric colors visible on your monitor as you visit these Psychedelic Minimalist sites. This is because a monitor screen makes its colors from pure light, whereas a printed book makes its colors from ink that reflects light. Ink color is *subtractive*—printed ink absorbs the colors you don't see and reflects the colors you do see. When primary print colors (cyan, magenta, yellow) mix, they result in a muddy brown. In contrast, screen colors are *additive*. When the primary screen colors (red, green, blue) mix, they make a pure white light. Screen colors and print colors actually exist in different color spaces, called *gamuts*. These color gamuts overlap somewhat, but there will always be some extreme screen colors that don't translate to print, and vice versa.

All this is academic to anyone who has translated between RGB (screen) color and CMYK (print) color. (The K in the acronym represents black, a necessary fourth color since cyan, magenta, and yellow don't actually combine to make true black.) Many web designers avoid extreme RGB screen colors that fall outside of the CMYK print color gamut. They believe these colors are gaudy and unnatural, since they don't normally appear in the real world of subtractive or reflective color. Yet Psychedelic Minimalist designers mine these extreme screen colors for their rich vibrancy and luminous sheen.

Bright "Screen" Colors for Navigation Elements

Because minimalist layouts purposefully inhibit a lot of background color, a natural place for color to appear is in navigation elements, such as link lists, link rollovers, main menus, submenus, and "you are here" wayfinding headers. Navigation color can be applied subtly or extremely, for purely decorative effect or to add layers of meaning.

In the New Media Initiatives section of the Walker Art Center site, everything is grayscale except the magenta link colors, the white on magenta header text, and the lime wiki page actions (**Figure 4.1**). Even the favicon logo (the tiny image that appears in the browser address field) is magenta. Rolling over a magenta link turns the link black and surrounds it with a

Figure 4.1 newmedia.walkerart.org/nmiwiki

magenta background. These two bright colors (magenta and lime) are enough to enliven an otherwise gray and somber page. The large dashes also add a bit of playfulness.

At olofsdotter.com, the system of graduated link colors (from red to black) indicates the relative newness of the project being linked (**Figure 4.2**). Bright red links lead to the freshest projects, while black links lead to the oldest projects. The links are arranged from freshest to oldest, creating a graduated cascade down the page. This playful system adds color as well as an extra layer of meaning to the navigation.

The site for the New Museum uses a different bright color for each of its main sections. On the site's home page, rolling over each section's name reveals its color (**Figure 4.3**). On the first page of each section, the name of the section in

the menu remains colored, and a submenu strip appears in the same color scheme (**Figure 4.4**). A colored square around any submenu section indicates you are in that section. Rolling over any submenu link surrounds it with a colored square, providing user feedback by indicating the link's function. Once you have clicked beyond the front page, rolling over any section name in the main menu reveals its color and its submenu strip, so you can go directly to any subsection from any page on the site.

This navigation scheme is intuitive and usable; no functionality has been sacrificed at the altar of psychedelia. The bright and unique colors of each section actually enhance functional navigation, because they distinguish the sections from each other and make wayfinding easy.

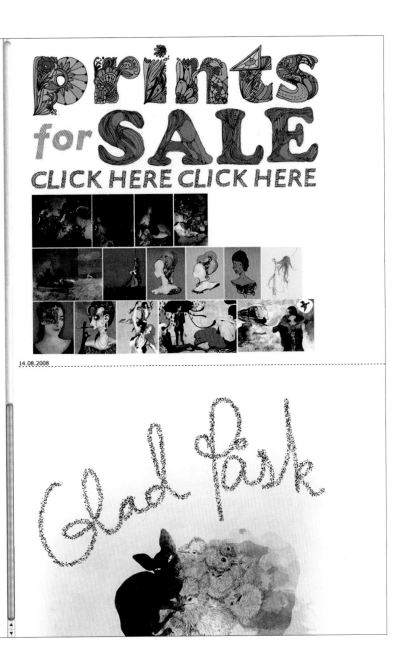

14.08.2008

Figure 4.2 olofsdotter.com

Figure 4.3 newmuseum.org

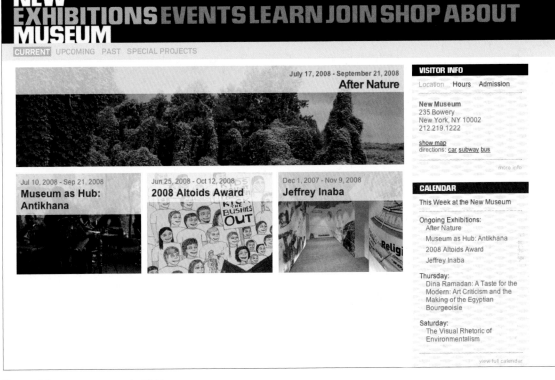

Figure 4.4 newmuseum.org/exhibitions

2	C	H	M	R	W
2000	c.i.	heavy.mp3	Made In Arnhem 2002	reclame	w123
2001	C60	Helios 80	Made In Arnhem 2005	redrum I	Wasylewski
2002	car	Helium	magazine	redrum II	water
2003	casa	Helium Ballooning	mainz	Reigerstraat	waterrocket I
2004	Catalogtree	hro	manned spaceflight	rocket	waterrocket II
2005	catalogtree	huisstijl	map	rocket science	weaving
2006	catalogus		media	rome	weblog
2007	chair	I	Men's Health	rotterdam	website
2008	chart	i-pod	mental map	Rotterdam 2001	website NEXT architects
	close	I.D. magazine	Mercedes	rubber stamp	Werkplaats Typografie
4	close encounters	IDEA magazine	Metropolis magazine	RuG	WIRED
	Close Encounters 3	index	mingus		Witte de With
40	Close Encounters Leader	infographic	modular origami	S	woodtype
400	Close Encounters Ypenburg	infographics	Monadnock	Sales Tax Rates	workshop
	Close Encounters Ypenburg 2	infoporn	Monadnock Poster	sample	worst
7	company	information design	Monopolis	sample aviation	Wurst
	company logo	Ingo	Monopolis-Antwerpen	sample chemistry	Würstchen
7x11	concrete	Ingo Offermanns	Monopolis Antwerpen	sample electronica	
7x11 advertisements	copycopy.mp3	inspiration	mp3	sample guns	Y
7x11 advertisements I	corporate identity	International	museum	sample plane	
7x11 corporate identity	Coster 1.0	interview	Museum Kurhaus Kleve	sample tachographs	YDU corporate identity
7x11 invitations (A3)	Coster 2.0	invitation	music	sample type	Year in Ideas
7x11 invitations I	cULTUUR 1	it is not going to stop	music machine	San Francisco	Ypenburg
7x11 invitations II	cULTUUR 2			schets	
7x11 posters I		J	N	Schoolstraat	Z
7x11 posters II	D	Joris Maltha		Scott Daddich	
7x11 posters III	Dag van de Ouderen	juul		screenprint	zefir7
7x11 website	Daniel Gross			Seed Magazine	
		K		Seed Magazine	
				SETI	
				shockwave	

Figure 4.5 catalogtree.net rolling over the year 2005

Cyan, Magenta, Yellow, and Black

One way to achieve a vibrant palette is to translate CMYK print colors into the RGB color gamut. Cyan, magenta, and yellow always wind up being brighter and more iridescent than they are in print. Several sites incorporate this CMYK scheme, although the actual screen colors they use vary slightly from site to site.

The main page for catalogtree.com is simply a long list of key phrases. Each phrase links to a project associated with that phrase. Rolling over a calendar year highlights all the phrases associated with that year in brilliant CMY (**Figure 4.5**). Rolling over any single phrase changes the color of that phrase and highlights all other associated phrases. Once a project is visited, its rollover color (cyan, magenta, or yellow) remains visible as a visited link color (**Figure 4.6**).

Drabber link colors might have receded into the otherwise grayscale layout. These bright CMY colors are integral to the success of Catalog Tree's navigation scheme because they are so prominently visible. Catalog Tree also uses the CSS text-decoration: line-through; property to effectively "cross out" previously visited links—an unorthodox but sensible approach in this context.

The CSS code for the page actually creates link subclasses labeled according the print colors they mean to approximate:

```css
a.cyan {
    color: #0099cc;
}
a.magenta {
    color: #ff00cc;
}
a.yellow {
    color: #ffff00;
}
```

ct

Catalogtree
Schoolstraat 35
6828 GT Arnhem
The Netherlands

telephone
+31 (0)26 3895655
faxmachine
+31 (0)26 3637252

--> go to index
--> send email
--> about

2

2000
2001
2002
2003
2004
2005
2006
2007
2008

4

40
400

7

7x11
7x11 advertisements
7x11 advertisements I
7X11 corporate identity
7x11 invitations (A3)
7x11 invitations I
7x11 invitations II
7x11 posters I
7x11 posters II
7x11 posters III
7x11 website

A

A325
about
about
affiche
aircraft carrier
Amsterdam
animatie
animation
Antwerpen
Architect magazine
Architect magazine '08
architecten
architects
Architecture
Arnhem
art
Artist
artist in residence
artoteek
Artoteek Den Haag
attention
audio
autocollider

B

baby
Ballooning
Basketball Talent
berserk
Biennale
bird
blog
boek
bomposter
book
Boompjes

C

c.i.
C60
car
casa
Catalogtree
catalogtree
catalogus
chair
chart
close
close encounters
Close Encounters 3
Close Encounters Leader
Close Encounters Ypenburg
Close Encounters Ypenburg 2
company
company logo
concrete
copycopy.mp3
corporate identity
Coster 1.0
Coster 2.0
cULTUUR 1
cULTUUR 2

D

Dag van de Ouderen
Daniel Gross
day and night
De Boompjes
De Paviljoens
den haag
Desalination
deserve
diagram
die hard
diplomats
Dirk Barnett
DNA
Doornbosch
drugs
DWIAWHGI
Dziga

E

e-zine
E.T.
Eindexamen 2000
Elten
encounters
Energy Market Europe
ESPN magazine
exhibition
exhibition

F

fashion
fellows
FGA swiss
Figures on Speed
film
film festival
filmpje I
filmpje II
filmpje III

H

heavy.mp3
Helios 80
Helium
Helium Ballooning
hro
huisstijl

I

i-pod
I.D. magazine
IDEA magazine
index
infographic
infographics
infoporn
information design
Ingo
Ingo Offermanns
inspiration
International
interview
invitation
it is not going to stop

J

Joris Maltha
juul

K

katalogbaum
Katharina
Katharina Grosse
key magazine
klick
Knoxcounty Nepotism
Knoxville voice
Kodak
kolpa
kosmos
krant

L

language
launch
leader
lecture
lecture at casa
lecture at FH-Mainz
lecture at ft 23
leisure
Leuker kunnen we t niet maken
Liesbeth Doornbosch
lofvers
Lofvers van Bergen Kolpa Architects
logo
loop
LUST
lvbk
LvBK IAB Rotterdam
LvBK invitation cards
LvBK Prix de Rome

M

Made In Arnhem 2002
Made In Arnhem 2005
magazine
mainz
manned spaceflight
map
media
Men's Health
mental map
Mercedes
Metropolis magazine
mingus
modular origami
Monadnock
Monadnock Poster
Monopolis
Monopolis - Antwerpen
Monopolis Antwerpen
mp3
museum
Museum Kurhaus Kleve
music
music machine

N

nearest neighbour
Nearest Neighbour
neon
nerve
New York
New York Times
newspaper
NEWWORK
next Architects
Nijmegen
nimitz
noise
nozzle
NYT CITIES
NYT databox

O

Offermanns
On Going

P

paper
parking
Parking Garage
parking violation
piepschuim
plaatsmaken
Plaatsmaken
Plaatsmaken Invitation
PLANYC
PM-NEON
post it
post-it
poster
postitposter
postscript
prix

R

reclame
redrum I
redrum II
Reigerstraat
rocket
rocket science
rome
rotterdam
Rotterdam 2001
rubber stamp
RuG

S

Sales Tax Rates
sample
sample aviation
sample chemistry
sample electronica
sample guns
sample plane
sample tachographs
sample type
San Francisco
schets
Schoolstraat
Scott Daddich
screenprint
Seed Magazine
Seed Magazine
SETI
shockwave
shop
signage
signage system
site specific
situation room.mp3
slide projector
snelweg
sound
SPD poster
speer bullets
sport
spraypaint
Stadsblokken
statistics
statistics
ster
studio
Super high way
swarm
system
systemantics

T

T-Shirt
tachographs
Tag
talkshow
talkshow 03-09-07
Ted Felen
test
the wedding.mp3
thijs gadiot
transurban
transurban
transurban (indices 1-3)
transurban (indices 4-5)
transurban (map 1-

W

w123
Wasylewski
water
waterrocket I
waterrocket II
weaving
weblog
website
website NEXT architects
Werkplaats Typografie
WIRED
Witte de With
woodtype
workshop
worst
Wurst
Würstchen

Y

YDU corporate identity
Year in Ideas
Ypenburg

Z

zefir7

Figure 4.6 catalogtree.net after visiting some links

```
Brussels (November 17 - December 2, 2007)
Jonctions / Verbindingen 10: Tracks in electr(on)ic fields
NL | FR

                                        About VJ10

Around us, magnetic        Tracks in electr(on)ic fields, gestures transformed into data,
fields resonate            codes that set bodies in motion, prescriptions that ask to be
unseen waves               interpreted. Pretended or real identities spread like viruses as
                           they are carried across networks by (un)controlable,
E-Traces                   commercialised and personalised information services, inhabiting
Mutual Motions             borders and embodying rumours.

Read Feel Feed Real        Opening November 24, La Bellone, 14:00 - 17:00
Participants
Places                     Verbindingen/Jonctions image galleries:
About VJ10                     • Preparation
About Constant                 • Saturday 17/11
                               • Saturday 24/11
Timetable                      • Sunday 25/11
Practical information          • Wednesday 28/11
                               • Thursday 29/11
Support                        • Friday 30/11
                               • Saturday 01/12
                               • Sunday 02/12

                           The interdisciplinary festival Jonctions/Verbindingen is at its
                           tenth edition. On location at La Bellone, Constant proposes a
                           series of reflections on our bodily, psychological and formal
                           relationship to technology. Following four parallel threads,
                           Verbindingen/Jonctions mixes electronic music, free
                           distribution, software creation, playful experimentation,
                           sociological survey, electronic cooking, experimental archiving
                           and techno-performance. What traces do technologies leave on us,
                           and how do we in return leave imprints on that technology? How
                           can we imagine other readings of the 'codified movements' we
                           perform vis-a-vis technology? How do we act around machines, and
                           can we shift away from repetitive strain, to gestures that
                           practice, point and probe?

                           This edition of Jonctions is put together in collaboration with
                           artist Michel Cleempoel (E-Traces), music programmer Yves
                           Poliart (Around us…), curator Bettina Knaup (video library) and
                           music, theatre and circus stage director Virginie Jortay
                           (production).

                           About Verbindingen/Jonctions:

                           Verbindingen/Jonctions (V/J), is an annual multidisciplinary
                           festival organised by Constant. It combines high-, low- and no-
                           tech strategies from utopian, contemporary, traditional and
                           tribal cultures with open standards, free licenses, feminism and
                           queer theories. Because we are interested in the space between
                           thinking and doing, the festival offers radio makers, artists,
                           software programmers, academics, Linux users, interface
                           designers, urban explorers, performance artists, technicians,
                           lawyers and others an occasion to experience each other's
                           practice, and share their interests with a broad public of
                           visitors.
```

Figure 4.7 data.constantvzw.org/vj10

These hexadecimal values are not mathematically equivalent to pure CMY values. For example, the web-safe color closest to actual print magenta is 009966. Fortunately, this mathematical discrepancy doesn't really matter, since the CMYK and RGB gamuts don't perfectly correspond anyway. The goal is simply to choose three CMY-ish colors that correspond to each other in the context of the site.

The VJ10 Festival page at constantvzw.org also uses a CMYK color scheme, with additional lime green characters (abstract dashes, parentheses, and question marks) for added background texture (**Figure 4.7**). These additional background characters subtly embody the theme of the festival, which is about invisible electronic traces.

The web site for Galerie Eva Presenhuber substitutes gray for black and foregoes magenta altogether, using only cyan and yellow (**Figure 4.8**). (Their cyan is #02c6ff and their yellow is #ffa800). The yellow appears only as a rollover color. The site's colors are meant to correspond with the art gallery's print advertisements in *ArtForum* magazine (**Figure 4.9**). In both contexts, this Psychedelic Minimalist approach is simultaneously elegant and electric. Regardless of which artist is currently having a show at the gallery, each artist is represented equally in the gallery's "house" style (**Figure 4.10**).

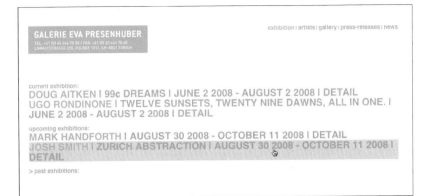

Figure 4.8 www.presenhuber.com

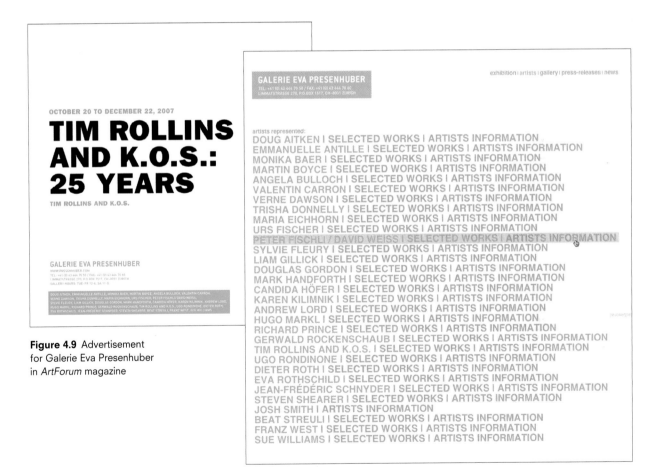

Figure 4.9 Advertisement for Galerie Eva Presenhuber in *ArtForum* magazine

Figure 4.10 www.presenhuber.com/en/artists.html

Art from code - Generator.x

Generator.x is a conference and exhibition examining the current role of software and generative strategies in art and design. [Read more...]

home | generator.x | beyond the screen | del.icio.us feed
about | contact

---

24 JAN - 2 FEB, 2008
CLUB TRANSMEDIALE / [DAM]

Generator.x 2.0: Beyond the screen is a workshop and exhibition about digital fabrication and generative systems, presented in collaboration with Club Transmediale and [DAM] Berlin.

24 Jan » Public presentations #1
28 Jan » Public presentations #2
01 Feb » Audiovisual concerts
02 Feb » Exhibition opening

BLOG CATEGORIES

+ BEAUTY OF NUMBERS (45)
+ CALLS / INFO (21)
+ COMP. ARCHITECTURE (15)
+ COMPUTATIONAL DESIGN (113)
+ DIGITAL FABRICATION (16)
+ GENERATIVE ART (163)
+ NEWS (57)
+ PEOPLE & PLACES (120)
+ PERFORMATIVE SOFTWARE (43)
+ SOUND WORKS (31)
+ TEXTS & THEORY (81)
+ TOOLS & CODE (80)
+ VIDEO (8)

+ BROWSE BY TAGS

SEARCH GENERATOR.X

[   ] [Search]

» Generator.x on Flickr

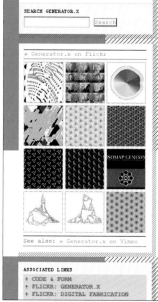

See also: » Generator.x on Vimeo

ASSOCIATED LINKS

+ CODE & FORM
+ FLICKR: GENERATOR.X
+ FLICKR: DIGITAL FABRICATION

» More than Just Pretty Pictures: Golan's Questions for Generative Artists

TAGS: No Tags

[Dear Colleagues,
Several of you have contacted me requesting that I post the "Three Questions for Generative Artists" that I posed to the audience during my lecture last week. (I state, for the record, that I don't have the answers, and I'm as perplexed/guilty as anyone else). Here they are.– Sincerely yours, Golan]

Marshall McLuhan stated, in 1964: "The medium is the message." Assuming we agree with this premise, in the way McLuhan intended it (as developed in his book *Understanding Media*), I posed the following questions concerning generative art:

0. So, with our generative artworks: what kinds of meanings are we making? In other words, what sorts of messages do generative artworks communicate, not *through* their medium, but *as* a medium?

1. How can generative strategies, which are designed to produce (or reflect) infinite variations, yield forms which nonetheless feel inevitable (i.e. which do not feel arbitrary)? Or is arbitrariness the point — the message of the medium? Here, I showed Jim Campbell's *"Formula for Computer Art"* (2001). As an illustration of different approaches on the spectrum between 'arbitrary' and 'motivated' generative designs, I contrasted Mark Napier's *"Black & White"* Carnivore client (2005), and Natalie Jeremijenko's *"Live Wire"* project (1994), both of which visualize network traffic. Both of these artworks subscribe to Campbell's Formula, but with very different results.

2. How can generative strategies tap into richer *perceptual* spaces? What other meaning-making potentials are latent in computational abstraction? Can we generalize the idea of generative *form*? Here, I showed Karl Sims' *"Evolved Virtual Creatures"* (1994). These creatures have extremely simple *forms* (rarely more elaborate than a couple of rectangular blocks) — but highly evocative, generatively-evolved *behaviors* which address our perception in a very rich way.

3. How can generative strategies tap into richer *conceptual* spaces, without sacrificing the experiential aesthetics of abstraction? Assuming we value abstraction for its powerful ability to address our perceptual and aesthetic senses (as I do), how can we expand the conceptual scope of generative art? Put another way, how can generative strategies activate further dimensions of our *psychology* (beyond retinal experience), such as our imaginations, symbolic [Jungian] minds, or unconscious minds? Here, I presented Jason Salavon's *"Form Study #1"* (2005). This project taps into rich cultural psychological territory, and provokes our imaginations, without (I claim) sacrificing generativity or abstract formalism in the slightest.

+del.icio.us | +digg

golan on Wednesday, October 5th, 2005 at 03:10. Filed under Generative art, Texts & theory. You can leave a response, or trackback from your own site.

---

7 RESPONSES TO "MORE THAN JUST PRETTY PICTURES: GOLAN'S QUESTIONS FOR GENERATIVE ARTISTS"

1. watz, October 6th, 2005 at 12:10

Having thought about your questions for a while, it seems to me that you are looking for a more functional form of generative art. But the works of Sims and Jeremijenko that you quote would usually not be classed as generative art. Even though they have a generative component, they fit well into other canons of electronic art (i.e. alife art or simply alife research in the case of Sims, or interactive art in the case of Jeremijenko). Savalon's form study I see as ironic, and not really addressing the generation of form. That's certainly not a bad thing, I like the project but I wouldn't see it as explaining much about generative art as such.

Figure 4.11 generatorx.no

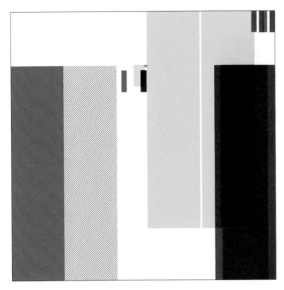

Figure 4.12 Background .gif of the page in Figure 4.11

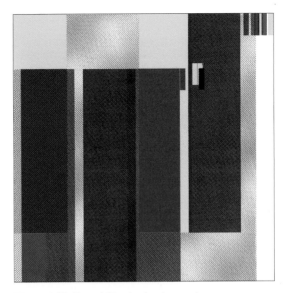

Figure 4.13 One of 10 other background .gifs from generatorx.no

Neon Patterns as Ornamental Architecture

Some Psychedelic Minimalist designers often use bright screen colors in abstract patterns as background ornamentation. These patterns never overwhelm or overtake the minimal grid structure of their sites. The patterns are not freeform, intuitive layout schemes; nor are they open, fullscreen baroque compositions. They are merely subtle embellishments that contribute to the to psychedelic side of the psychedelic-minimalist balance.

generatorx.no is an extreme example of neon ornamental architecture (**Figure 4.11**). The site has 10 different background patterns (**Figures 4.12** and **4.13**). These intricate, cross-hatched, vertically tiling patterns are applied generatively. Every 30 seconds a new background pattern is assigned to all the pages of the site. However, the background patterns

don't swap out while you are reading a page. They only change when you visit a new page or refresh an old page, provided 30 seconds have transpired since the last time you changed pages. The 10 background patterns all share a similar color scheme. They are designed to seamlessly collage with other tiling, cross-hatched patterns in the foreground layout of each page.

Surfing generatorx.no can be subtly unsettling. Each page of the site looks more or less the same, but as you backtrack through the site, you notice that pages you have visited are slightly changed—an appropriate effect for a website about software-modulated design. Functionally, generatorx.no is really just a standard weblog, but visually it is anything but standard. An ingenious combination of textures and colors elevate this site to lush, vibrant extremes of Psychedelic Minimalism.

Figure 4.14 pbs.org/art21 at 1024-pixels wide

Background Killer: Neon Diagonals, Dots, Gradients, and Patterns

Because Psychedelic Minimalist style is a lot like Late(st) Modernist style, but with bright colors added, the dotted and diagonal backgrounds that work for Late(st) Modernism also work for Psychedelic Minimalism. All you need to do is change the colors from grayscale to neon. generatorx.no is an extreme and complex example of psychedelic diagonal backgrounds, but you can always apply yours more subtly.

Neon-colored gradients are another way to kill Psychedelic Minimalist backgrounds. The web site for the PBS television series art21 uses a different gradient background for each section. The gradient background colors match the wayfinding and navigation colors of their respective sections. If visitors' windows are 1024-pixels wide, they see only part of the gradient background (**Figure 4.14**). If their windows are 1280-pixels wide, they see more of the background (**Figure 4.15**). The gradient background effectively kills the extra right-hand negative space while enhancing the color scheme of the content area.

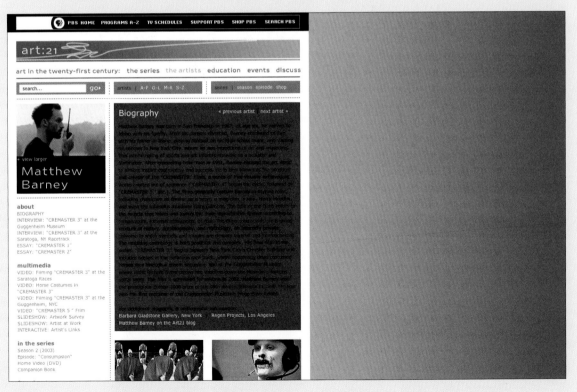

Figure 4.15 pbs.org/art21/artists/barney at 1280-pixels wide

Figure 4.16
lifelongfriendshipsociety.com/site/
news.php at 1152-pixels wide

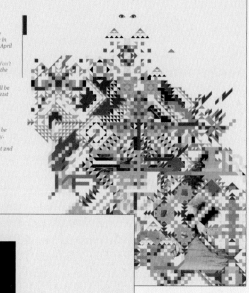

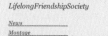

Figure 4.17 lifelongfriendshipsociety.com/site/
archive.php?id_project=93&image=2 at 1152-pixels wide

The design portfolio of Lifelong Friendship Society kills its right-hand background with an abstract, non-tiling, Santa Fe-esque quilting pattern. The pattern takes up more space in the site's News section, because the news column is narrow (**Figure 4.16**). It takes up less space in the portfolio section, because the portfolio content area is wider (**Figure 4.17**). The color scheme of the pattern purposefully matches the color scheme of the submenu links in the portfolio section.

Uses

The Psychedelic Minimalist style is the ideal combination of elegance and fun, a bit like the playful little sister of Late(st) Modernist style. It is suitable for any product or service that is supposed to be fun, but not off-the-chain insane. It works for products and services that are meant to appear overtly "creative," but not irresponsibly anarchic.

Psychedelic Minimalism would be a good web design style to use for an arts organization, such as an art gallery, art museum, or grant-funding foundation. The minimalism says, "We are professionals." The psychedelia adds, "We are also creative." In addition, any academic institution related to art, design, or visual communication would be a good candidate for Psychedelic Minimalist design. For example, the ideal web site for an undergraduate design department would appear well designed from a modernist perspective, but would also have a bit of psychedelic flair. This balance lets prospective students know that they will learn how to design professionally and "properly," while still experiencing a needful dose of experimentation and play.

Because Psychedelic Minimalist style retains the grid structure of Late(st) Modernism, it is an ideal style for a catalog site, but for a younger demographic. The psychedelic colors could be shifted to muted pastels for a kid's clothing site like Gymboree, or ramped up to bright neons for a girl's accessory site like Sanrio.

● ● ●

Mashing-up two contradictory design approaches like minimalism and psychedelia seems like the result of a provocative thought experiment: Pick two extreme opposites and try to hybridize them. In the case of Psychedelic Minimalist style, the resultant hybrid allows both extremes to shine without muddying them in the middle by compromise. Bright screen colors stand out all the more because they appear as unexpected guests in an otherwise restrained compositional scenario. The stage is set for a grayscale evening, when suddenly the CMYK posse bum rushes the show! Sometimes strange bedfellows make the best bedfellows.

DOT MATRIX

N. A DENSE GRID OF DOTS OR PINS USED TO FORM CHARACTERS OR DESIGNS, AS BY SOME COMPUTER PRINTERS AND VISUAL DISPLAY UNITS.

–THE AMERICAN HERITAGE DICTIONARY

05 | *DOT MATRIX STYLE*

Most design approaches are radically affected by the typefaces they employ, and Dot Matrix style is no exception. It begins with monospaced typography—either typewriter text or bitmap "computer" text—and proceeds in a homemade, do-it-yourself, low-tech fashion. Dot Matrix sites are constructed from the same raw digital materials as other web sites, including XHTML, CSS, Flash, and so on; but they are intentionally made to look as if they were published in someone's basement, evoking an overt nostalgia for amateur press fanzines and online bulletin board systems.

Influences

Dot matrix printers ruled the cheap desktop publishing era of the 1980s. They achieved their results by physically stamping ink on paper. Their output was glitchy in a hybrid digital-analog way. Their letterforms were based on a grid of dots that were often visible as a result of unevenly applied ink. Horizontal borders were often created by simply typing a row of dashes, plus signs, pound signs, percentage signs, or asterisks. These are the visual hallmarks of low budget, homemade publications printed on dot matrix printers.

Prior to computers, D.I.Y. fanzines (for science fiction, rock music, punk music, and fringe subcultures) were created on typewriters and then copied on ditto machines, and later on Xerox copiers. The more pages your magazine had, the more expensive it was to copy. Since finances were usually tight for these amateur publishers, layout space was always an issue. One way to overcome the problem was to cram as much information into as tight a space as possible, all separated by borders of (you guessed it) dashes, dots, asterisks, and so on.

The command-line menus of early online Bulletin Board Systems (BBSes) and the 8-bit, text-only menu options of Atari 2600 game systems also influence the Dot Matrix style. Both menu systems were limited to non-anti-aliased, bitmap digital typography. Graphics were crude at best, often achieved by arranging letters to make rudimentary visual forms (the practice known as *ASCII art*). Like the typewritten fanzines, space was a premium because each screen could only hold so much information before the user had to invoke the next screen. Tightly scrunched rows of text separated by dashed borders were the norm.

GIVEN ITS "RETRO" INFLUENCES, DOT MATRIX STYLE COMES ACROSS AS INTENTIONALLY PLAYFUL AND SLIGHTLY NERDY—AN INSIDE WINK TO THOSE GEEKS WHO REMEMBER THE SUBCULTURE FANZINES AND PRE-WEB NET INTERFACES FROM BACK IN THE DAY.

Characteristics

Given its "retro" influences, Dot Matrix style comes across as intentionally playful and slightly nerdy—an inside wink to those geeks who remember the subculture fanzines and pre-web net interfaces from back in the day. The style's characteristics arise from its influences.

On the web there is no extra financial charge for multiple pages of text, so the practice of scrunching content becomes purposefully (and fetishistically) nostalgic. Cramming a bunch of content together in a particular way simply connotes a self-publishing D.I.Y. ethic. Nevertheless, on a content-rich news site where space is always a premium, Dot Matrix style can be practically applied in a clean and restrained manner to deliver a lot of information in a very serviceable and compact way.

Monospaced Type

Monospaced typography arose because certain systems (the typewriter and the 8-bit computer) were unable to render letterforms at different widths. Ideally, the letter *w* should take up more space than the letter *i*, but monospaced typefaces give each letter the same fixed width. Monospaced typefaces are less subtle and more obtrusive than variable-width typefaces, and because of this they are more readily associated with certain technological eras.

Monospaced typewriter type is easily achieved via CSS using one of the two browser-safe monospaced typefaces: Courier or Courier New. On the website abstraction-now.at, a full cascade of monospaced browser typefaces are specified:

```
font-family: "Andale Mono", "Lucida
Console", LucidaTypewriter, Courier,
monospace;
```

Andale Mono is available by default on Macintosh machines, so Macintosh users will see this font when viewing the site (**Figure 5.1**). Lucida Console is a default typeface on PCs, so most PC users will see Lucida Console when viewing the site. Finally, Courier is a default typeface on all operating systems, so Linux users will see that one. This complex cascade specification is an overly fancy way to approach the problem. The simple solution is to specify courier or "courier new" and then monospace.

The Abstraction Now links are arranged as if they are part of a command-line menu system short on screen space. There is an underscore between the first and last name of each artist listed in the link list, and double slashes separating the links. The palette is completely grayscale. The Abstraction Now logo is a .gif of an architectural, "techno" font. All of these details combine to connote a bygone era of old-school digital technology.

Monospaced bitmap typography, the digital typography associated with command-line interfaces, is achieved by using a bitmap typeface in Photoshop or Illustrator and saving the image of your words as a .gif, or by embedding a bitmap typeface in Flash. Bitmap faces should never be anti-aliased. They were designed with

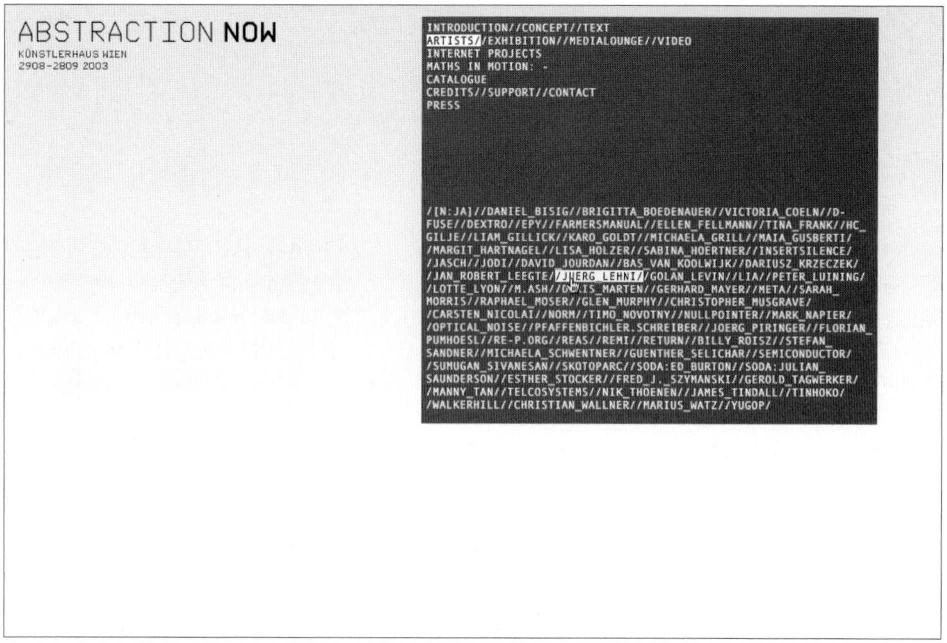

ABSTRACTION **NOW**
KÜNSTLERHAUS WIEN
2908-2809 2003

INTRODUCTION//CONCEPT//TEXT
ARTISTS//EXHIBITION//MEDIALOUNGE//VIDEO
INTERNET PROJECTS
MATHS IN MOTION: -
CATALOGUE
CREDITS//SUPPORT//CONTACT
PRESS

/[N:JA]//DANIEL_BISIG//BRIGITTA_BOEDENAUER//VICTORIA_COELN//D-
FUSE//DEXTRO//EPY//FARMERSMANUAL//ELLEN_FELLMANN//TINA_FRANK//HC_
GILJE//LIAM_GILLICK//KARO_GOLDT//MICHAELA_GRILL//MAIA_GUSBERTI/
MARGIT_HARTNAGEL//LISA_HOLZER//SABINA_HOERTNER//INSERTSILENCE/
/JASCH//JODI//DAVID_JOURDAN//BAS_VAN_KOOLWIJK//DARIUSZ_KRZECZEK/
/JAN_ROBERT_LEEGTE//JUERG_LEHNI//GOLAN_LEVIN//LIA//PETER_LUINING/
/LOTTE_LYON//M.ASH//DORIS_MARTEN//GERHARD_MAYER//META//SARAH_
MORRIS//RAPHAEL_MOSER//GLEN_MURPHY//CHRISTOPHER_MUSGRAVE/
/CARSTEN_NICOLAI//NORM//TIMO_NOVOTNY//NULLPOINTER//MARK_NAPIER/
/OPTICAL_NOISE//PFAFFENBICHLER.SCHREIBER//JOERG_PIRINGER//FLORIAN_
PUMHOESL//RE-P.ORG//REAS//REMI//RETURN//BILLY_ROISZ//STEFAN_
SANDNER//MICHAELA_SCHWENTNER//GUENTHER_SELICHAR//SEMICONDUCTOR/
/SUMUGAN_SIVANESAN//SKOTOPARC//SODA:ED_BURTON//SODA:JULIAN_
SAUNDERSON//ESTHER_STOCKER//FRED_J._SZYMANSKI//GEROLD_TAGWERKER/
/MANNY_TAN//TELCOSYSTEMS//NIK_THOENEN//JAMES_TINDALL//TINHOKO/
/WALKERHILL//CHRISTIAN_WALLNER//MARIUS_WATZ//YUGOP/

Figure 5.1
abstraction-now.at/?artists

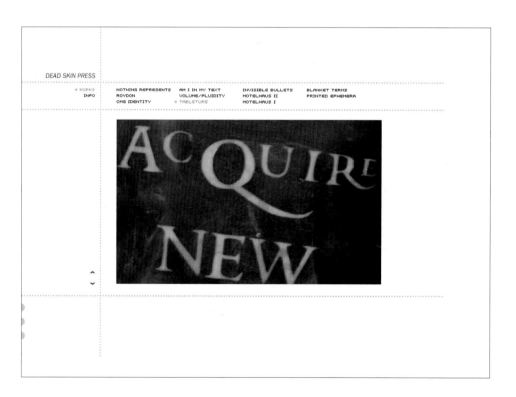

Figure 5.2
deadskinpress.com

their crisp, hard edges specifically not to need anti-aliasing.

The Dead Skin Press site uses bitmap typography in the form of .gifs, along with subtle dots that offset the menu and frame the content (**Figure 5.2**). The dots seem like physical perforations in the digital page. The menu typeface was specifically selected to not compete with the serif, ornate, Old Style typefaces featured in the content images.

Bonsaimai.de uses Flash to display its bitmap digital typography (**Figure 5.3**). Horizontal double-dash lines separate the main menu items, while single-dash lines separate the drop-down submenu items. If a link is made up of more than one word, underscores are used to connect the words. Like the Dead Skin Press site, bonsaimai.de foregoes intense content compression and instead opts for open negative space. Both sites subtly and minimally apply Dot Matrix style. At bonsaimai.de, the combination of dashes and digital typography alone is enough to push the site in the Dot Matrix direction.

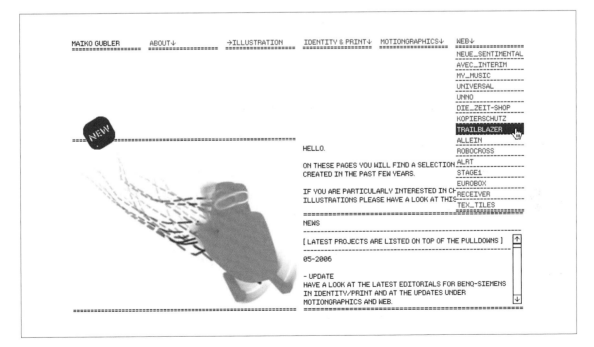

Figure 5.3 bonsaimai.de

MONDAY, 10 MAY 1976
DIR MEM INFO HIDE

15:54:22 ae

s m t w t f 01
02 03 04 05 06 07 08
09 10 11 12 13 14 15
16 17 18 19 20 21 22
23 24 25 26 27 28 29
30 31

RICKY, IRENE, MARC, RICHARD, CATHY, BERT, DIETER, MAUREEN
500K

---- --- --   ---- --- --
---- --- --   ---- --- --
---- --- --   ---- --- --
1978 APR 18   ---- --- --
---- --- --   ---- --- --
---- --- --   ---- --- --
2004 JAN 19   ---- --- --
2004 APR 17   ---- --- --
2016 NOV 02   ---- --- --
1980 JUN 15   1971 JAN 31
1980 JUN 14
2010 MAR 18
2041 MAR 19
1992 JUN 17
---- --- --
1988 NOV 24
---- --- --

Figure 5.4 tex-server.org/3/

The tex-server 3 site (an archived, 2004 version of tex-server.org) uses Flash to push the command-line menu metaphor to its extreme (**Figure 5.4**). Rolling over and clicking on links generates audible, "computery" blips and bleeps. Like a true command-line interface, keystrokes actually control functionality. Typing a *d* (for Directory) expands and contracts the menu; typing an *h* (for Hide) causes the menu to disappear altogether. The site's content is displayed fullscreen behind the menu system. Hiding the menu leaves you with a screen full of pure content. The menu links are cryptically arranged according to a surreal chronological scheme that enhances the site's conceptual exploration of memory.

Dashes and Dots for Borders and Visual Texture

We have already found dashes and dots used for borders in some of the previous examples cited in this chapter. In addition to simply separating content, these borders add either a "typewritery" fanzine connotation or a command-line aura. Dashes and dots can also be applied abundantly and abstractly to other areas of the page, adding further visual texture.

The Maths In Motion subsite at abstraction-now.at situates its header text in an abstract grid of simple black dots (**Figure 5.5**). These dots effectively define the right edge of the content area without resorting to a vertical line or a solid background color. This matrix of dots also effectively alludes to the dot matrix era of the '80s.

close

MATHS IN MOTION

MATHEMATISCHE KONZEPTE IM EXPERIMENTELLEN FILM UND VIDEO

29.08. - 27.09.2003
KÜNSTLERHAUSKINO WIEN

eine **Veranstaltung von**   sixpack film

Programm

Installation - Island
Credits

| 1| FR 29.08 | 3| FR 05.09 | 5| FR 12.09 | 7| FR 19.09 | 9| FR 26.09 |
| 2| SA 30.08 | 4| SA 06.09 | 6| SA 13.08 | 8| SA 20.09 | 10| SA 27.09 |

Der Titel der Film/Videoschau ist eine Paraphrase auf
ein einflussreiches Manifest des ungarischen
Bauhausmeisters und Konstruktivisten László Moholy-
Nagy, das posthum erstmals 1947 publiziert wurde:
„Vision in Motion". „Der strenge" Geist der Mathematik
wird ostentativ an die Stelle der „künstlerischen"
Vision gesetzt, wobei der Beweis angetreten wird, dass
künstlerischer Anspruch und mathematische Konzeption
und Präzision durchaus keine Gegensätze sind.

Abb.   MATHS IN MOTION begleitet und erweitert die

Figure 5.5 abstraction-now.at/MATHS_IN_MOTION/

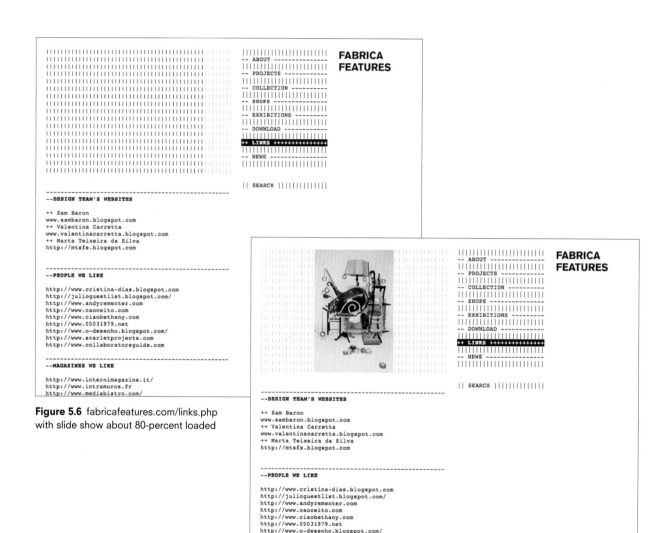

Figure 5.6 fabricafeatures.com/links.php
with slide show about 80-percent loaded

Figure 5.7 fabricafeatures.com/links.php with slide show fully loaded

The Fabrica Features site uses a row of vertical hashes to separate its menu items. Horizontal plus signs indicate the "you are here" state of a link, while horizontal dashes indicate that a link is clickable.

The vertical hashes are repeated in the slide show content area to the left of the menu. As the slide show loads, the gray hashes gradually turn to black, indicating the percentage of the slide show that has loaded (**Figure 5.6**). Once the slide show is fully loaded, the gray hashes remain in the background, demarcating the slide-show content area for images that aren't large enough to fill the whole area (**Figure 5.7**).

The simple repetition of hashes, dashes, and plus signs throughout the page add visual unity. These typewritery embellishments make the site feel like a homemade publication. On the other hand, the use of abundant white space, gridded alignment, and a sans-serif logotype reveal a modernist design mind at work. This hybridization of Dot Matrix style and Late(st) Modern style results in a quirky, original, but still very functional visual solution.

Compressed Layout

Dot Matrix style is ideal for compressing a lot of content into a small space. Dashed borders mean less negative space has to be used between rows and columns, so text content can be piled and squeezed.

The website for the FILE electronic arts festival achieves its content compression cleanly, efficiently, and elegantly, without sacrificing legibility (**Figure 5.8**). Ideally you wouldn't typeset an entire article of body copy in a monospaced font, but the paragraphs on the FILE front page are only short blurbs, so they don't suffer from being set in Courier New. The monospaced font actually alludes to the fanzine style, subtly letting us know that the site's extreme compression is not accidental but intentional. There is a lot of information on this page, but it doesn't feel crowded. In lieu of dashed borders, plus signs are used as crosshatches to indicate the corners of each content area.

Figure 5.8 file.org.br

Animated, Dotted Logotype

Although Dot Matrix style logotype is usually monospaced, the design firm Universal Everything has created two noteworthy exceptions: an interactive logo for its video blog Everyone Forever, and a gorgeously dissipating logo for its video gallery Advanced Beauty.

The letters in the Everyone Forever logo are made up of hundreds of tiny dots (**Figure 5.9**). The logo seems strange but still fairly reserved...until you roll over it. The logo is actually an interactive Flash animation that disperses the dots in a morphing cloud as you move your mouse across the words (**Figure 5.10**). Once your mouse stops moving, the dots gradually settle like dust back into their original letterforms.

The Advanced Beauty logo is not interactive, but it is designed along a similar visual metaphor (**Figure 5.11**). Its letters are made of colorful dots, frozen in the act of dispersion. To the right of the logo, the dots seem to have taken on a life of their own—growing larger, breaking out of the grid, and escaping off the edge of the page. Some smaller dots have even migrated into the top menu tab.

The Everyone Forever and Advanced Beauty logos activate a static matrix of dots to achieve a vibrant, organic flow of pattern and color. Both logos break out of the Dot Matrix style to create a startling, original effect.

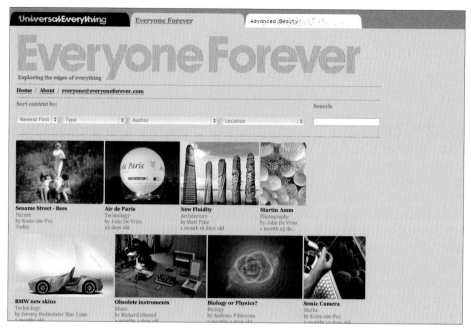

Figure 5.9 everyoneforever.com prior to logo rollover

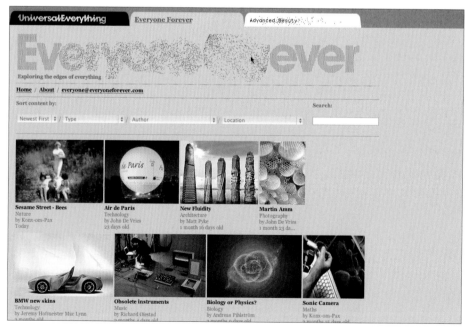

Figure 5.10 everyoneforever.com during logo rollover

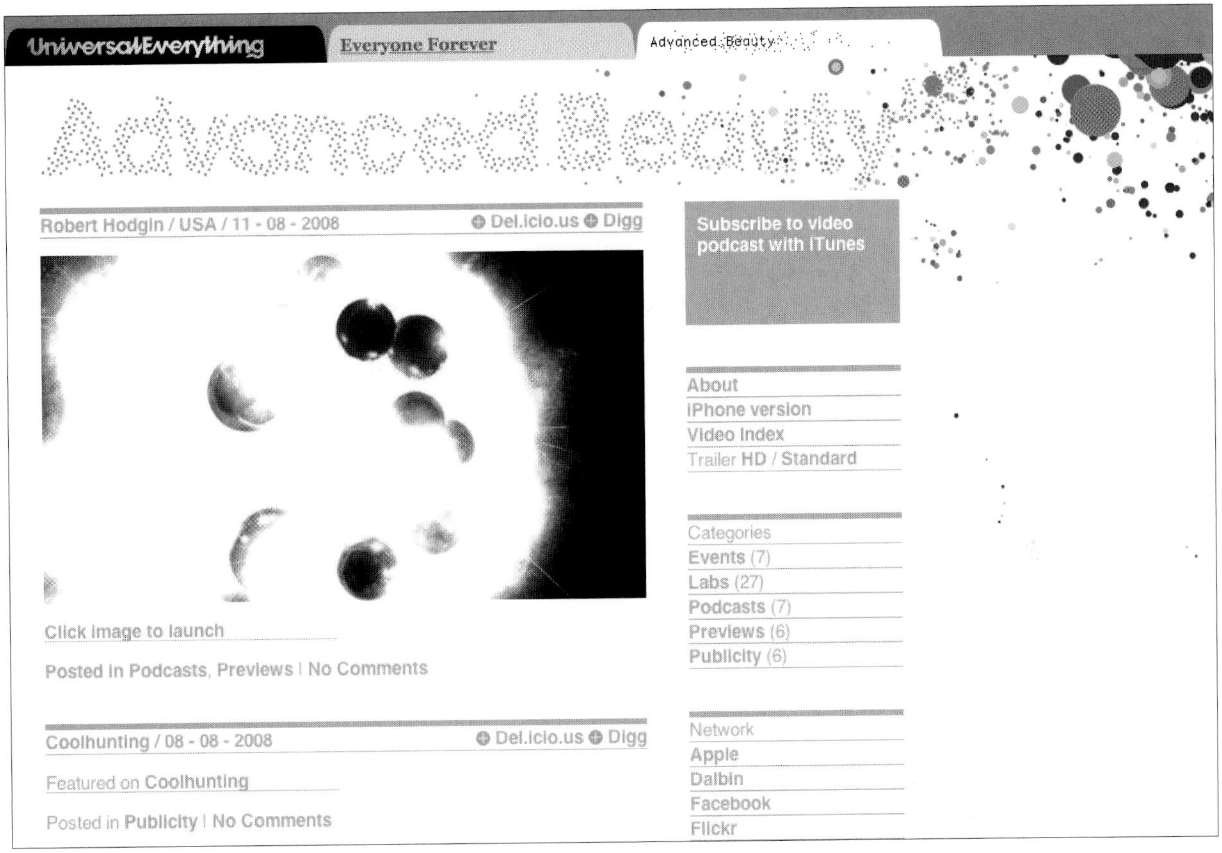

Figure 5.11 advancedbeauty.org

Background Killer: ASCII Abstraction

Since Dot Matrix style layouts are often compressed, one background-killer approach is simply to leave white any remaining noncontent background space. This arguably gives the page more room to breathe and creates interesting visual contrast.

But if the point of Dot Matrix style is to overcrowd the page, then a more extreme, purist way to kill background space is by filling it with abstract ASCII art: dots, dashes, symbols, and letters arranged to form patterns and images. This abstract text will admittedly compete with your content area text, and that confusion is often the point.

At spectatormag.net, the distinction between abstract background patterns and actual content is intentionally blurred because the content area itself is already quite abstract, and the abstract background patterns are created from content (**Figure 5.12**). The abstract ASCII background proceeds down and across the page. This approach is playful to the cryptic extreme. It celebrates the era of homemade fanzines when access to a typewriter and a copy machine inspired giddy, self-fulfilling experiments in self-publishing.

Figure 5.12 spectormag.net scrolling vertically

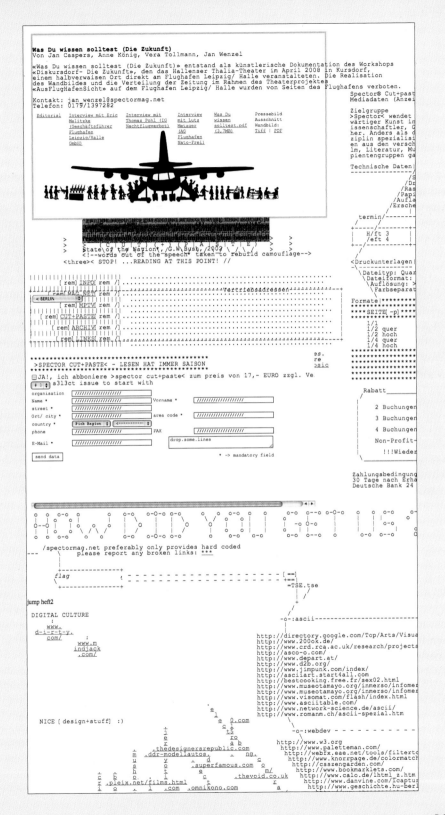

Was Du wissen solltest (Die Zukunft)
Von Jan Caspers, Anne König, Vera Tollmann, Jan Wenzel

«Was Du wissen solltest (Die Zukunft)» entstand als künstlerische Dokumentation des Workshops
«Diskursdorf- Die Zukunft», den das Hallenser Thalia-Theater im April 2008 in Kursdorf,
einem halbverwaisen Ort direkt am Flughafen Leipzig/ Halle veranstalteten. Die Realisation
des Wandbildes und die Verteilung der Zeitung im Rahmen des Theaterprojektes
«AusFlugHafenSicht» auf dem Flughafen Leipzig/ Halle wurden von Seiten des Flughafens verboten.

Kontakt: jan_wenzel@spectormag.net
Telefon: 0179/1397282

Editorial | Interview mit Eric Melitzke (Geschäftsführer Flughafen Leipzig/Halle GmbH) | Interview mit Thomas Pohl (IG Nachtflugverbot) | Interview mit Lutz Metzger IAG Flughafen Nato-Frei) | Was Du wissen solltest.pdf (3,7MB) | Pressebild Ausschnitt Wandbild: Tiff | PDF

Spector® Cut+past
Mediadaten (Anzei

Zielgruppe
>Spectork wendet
wärtiger Kunst in
issenschaftler, G
her. Anders als d
ziplin spezialisi
en aus den versch
lm, Literatur, Mu
pientengruppen ga

Technische Daten

              /S
              /Dr
              /Ras
              /Papi
              /Aufla
              /Ersche

termin/---------

| H/ft 3
| /eft 4

<Druckunterlagen

\Dateityp: Quar
\Dateiformat:
\Auflösung: >
\Farbseparat

Formate|*********
**********SEITE| -p|*
****

1/1
1/2 quer
1/2 hoch
1/4 quer
1/4 hoch

>
State Of the Nation/ /G.W.Bush/2002
<!--words out of the speech* taken to rebuild camouflage-->
<three>< STOP! ...READING AT THIS POINT! //

[rem] INFO| rem /|
[rem] MAG_NET| rem /|
< BERLIN
[rem] MP_TV| rem /|
[rem] CUT+PASTE| rem /|
[rem] ARCHIV| rem /|
[rem] LINKS| rem /|

Vertriebsadressen

Rabatt

/
2 Buchungen
3 Buchungen
4 Buchungen
Non-Profit-
!!!Wieder

>SPECTOR CUT+PASTE< - LESEN HAT IMMER SAISON
□ JA!, ich abboniere >spector cut+paste< zum preis von 17,- EURO zzgl. Ve
[# 1] s3l3ct issue to start with

organisation
Name *   Vorname *
street *
Ort/ city *   area code *
country *   Pick Region   <----------->
phone   FAX
E-Mail *   drop.some.lines

[send data]   * -> mandatory field

Zahlungsbedingung
30 Tage nach Erha
Deutsche Bank 24

/spectormag.net preferably only provides hard coded
          please report any broken links: ***

flag   [==]
                                               =TSE.tse

jump heft2

DIGITAL CULTURE
-o-:ascii----------------------
http://directory.google.com/Top/Arts/Visua
http://www.200ok.de/
http://www.crd.rca.ac.uk/research/projects
http://asco-o.com/
http://www.depart.at/
http://www.d2b.org/
http://www.jimpunk.com/index/
http://asciiart.start4all.com
http://bestcooking.free.fr/sex02.html
http://www.museotamayo.org/inmerso/infomer
http://www.museotamayo.org/inmerso/infomer
http://www.visomat.com/flash/index.html
http://www.asciitable.com/
http://www.network-science.de/ascii/
http://www.romanm.ch/ascii-spezial.htm

www.
d-i-r-t-y.
com/
www.m
indjack
.com/

NICE [design+stuff] :)

-o-:webdev - - - - - - - -
http://www.w3.org
http://www.paletteman.com/
http://webfx.eae.net/tools/filterto
http://www.knorrpage.de/colormatch
http://csszengarden.com/
http://www.bookmarklets.com/
http://www.calo.de/html_2.htm
http://www.danvine.com/Icapture
http://www.geschichte.hu-berl

.thedesignersrepublic.com
.ddr-modelautos.
.superfamous.com
.thevoid.co.uk
.pleix.net/films.html
.com .omnikono.com

Uses

Dot Matrix style is perfect for achieving a tongue-in-cheek, self-aware, retro-techno look. It is applicable for a computer science departmental web site (provided the computer science department doesn't take itself too seriously). It is applicable to any event, conference, or festival website celebrating digital art, Internet art, the history of the technology, the history of computing, the history of gaming, or any other technological topic.

In addition to these more specific uses, Dot Matrix style seems applicable to almost any online newspaper front page. It is a visually novel but practical and effective approach to presenting a lot of text in a small space. When applied conservatively, it need not overtly connote historical monospaced printing and display technologies. Courier type could be used for front-page blurbs, to be replaced by more legible type on secondary pages containing multi-paragraph articles.

● ● ●

You might think it would take more than the mere application of a monospaced typeface and a few dashes to constitute a recognizable visual style, but monospaced faces are so seldom used online, that when they are used they are immediately recognizable and associated with a certain historical aesthetic.

Why is a visual style that was more or less a hindrance only 20 years ago now hailed as desirably nostalgic? Because the coders and designers of today were the children of just yesterday, and when they think self-publishing, they recall typewriter fanzines and dot matrix printers. In Medieval times, technology changed slowly. You might still be using the same model plow your grandfather used. These days technology changes rapidly, and new technologies suggest new visual styles. Rapid technological churn can be exhausting and daunting. It's no wonder people take nostalgic comfort in the look and feel of old technologies, even if "old" only means 20 years ago. The former monospaced limitations of the Dot Matrix style are now the hallmark of its contemporary visual charm.

Welcome to the INTERNET. ...
ENJOY the RIDE.

—A BADLY ANIMATED .GIF, CIRCA 1996

06 | *1996 DIRT STYLE*

The early years of the World Wide Web saw a proliferation of very unattractive websites made by amateur designers. Rather than beginning with a visual mockup in Photoshop and coding their pages accordingly, most early web designers simply began with the HTML itself. Instead of striving to overcome the inherent limitations of the code, they let its limitations guide their design decisions. This approach often resulted in wall-to-wall screen text separated by cheesy beveled borders atop tiling animated .gif backgrounds of twinkling stars in "cyberspace."

This hobbyist homepage era lasted until corporations and more professional designers began designing web sites for profit. Thus began the reign of the corporate web. It flourished until the advent of "web 2.0" and social networking, when hobbyist designers were suddenly re-invited and thus empowered to make their own web logs.

This time around, the professional designers tried their best to keep the new influx of hobbyist designers from making "bad" designs. The professionals crafted good-looking, standards-compliant templates for bloggers to use. Then MySpace came along and ruined everything. Suddenly, we were thrust back in the design world of 1996 Dirt style.

What is 1996 Dirt style? In a nutshell, it's hobbyist-generated, hodge-podge, kitchen-sink, old-school design. The term comes from a lecture given by Internet artist Cory Arcangel in 2001. In that lecture, he described several design fundamentals of 1996 Dirt style:

1. Dirt-style projects must be nasty. Think fourth-generation VHS dubs, Xerox copies made with a cartridge low on toner, post-rap Vanilla Ice, or any car made in the '80s that ran on diesel. Now translate that into web design.

2. In case you haven't figured it out yet, designing websites is the same as designing brochures. Did you ever know a cool brochure designer? I didn't think so. Stop wasting time on web design. It's so 1997 and never was cool anyway. Try spending time on your ideas.

3. Your heroes are people who make airplane cockpits in their garage, turn their scanners into record players, recreate *Star Wars* in Legos, and port Tetris to the ColecoVision. Do you think they had time to learn Flash MX? So you shouldn't learn it either.

The obvious question remains: Why would you want to design a bad-looking site? You may not want to, but millions of MySpace hobbyist designers do, and there are actually a number of reasons, both ethical and commercial, that you might want to facilitate (or at least allow for) these endeavors. We'll talk about some of them in this chapter.

Influences

1996 Dirt style is influenced by the culture of homemade hobbyists, who, by the way, were adding idiosyncratic touches to their personal items well before 1996—sewing sequins on store-bought t-shirts and modifying assembly-line cars. It was only in 1996, with the first wave of web design, that hobbyists began applying their own personal digital embellishments to the noncommercial web.

1996 Personal Homepages

1996 Dirt style is greatly influenced by hobbyist-created personal home pages circa 1996. These pages were not yet blogs or even sites, but simply long, vertical scrolling pages full of links, text, images, animated under-construction .gifs, broken hit counters, and gaudy tiling backgrounds. Contemporary Dirt-style designers are influenced by the cheesy look of these early pages, without being wed to their old-school code.

1996 Dirt style can actually be fully standards-compliant, as demonstrated by Bruce Lawson's hilarious Dirt-style page for the CSS Zen Garden project (**Figure 6.1**). The layout and visual design of the page are accomplished via an external Cascading Style Sheet—proper separation of style and content—even though the style happens to be ridiculously improper.

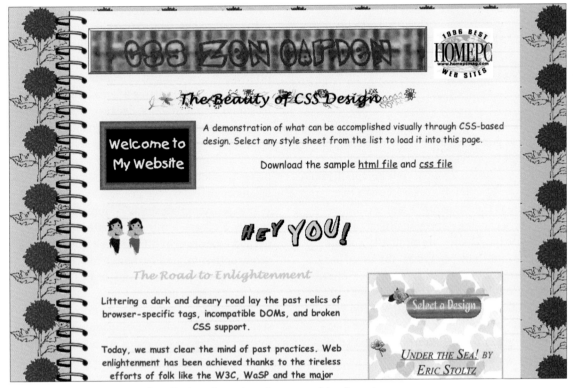

Figure 6.1 csszengarden.com/?cssfile=http://www.brucelawson.co.uk/zen/sample.css

Figure 6.2 a
blinged-out watch

Custom Cars

Custom car culture is the automotive counter-part of 1996 Dirt style. Modifying or "pimping" your ride is a way to display your personal, idio-syncratic design preferences. Although two cars may begin as the same make and model, no two custom cars are exactly identical.

1996 Dirt-style sites are similar to custom cars—two sites may begin with the same basic design template, but once they are customized, no two sites ever wind up looking exactly alike. The modifications are mostly superficial visual embellishments, whereas the under-the-hood functionality of Dirt-style sites remains stan-dard and similar across the board.

Bling Fashion

Bright, sparkly, shiny objects have always been a straightforward way to show personal flair and attract immediate attention (**Figure 6.2**). Whether "bling" is created using real gold and diamonds or gold paint and plastic is often irrelevant. Any normal object (such as a neck-lace, cell-phone case, or poodle collar) can be blinged-out. The digital equivalent of this phenomenon is sparkly .gif animations. As you will see, no 1996 Dirt-style image is safe from a healthy dose of blingification.

Characteristics

1996 Dirt style can be thought of as decidely *un*blogger and very pro-MySpace. When blog-gers decide to create a web log at blogger.com, they select from several well designed, premade visual templates (**Figure 6.3**). These official Blogger templates are designed by pro-fessional web designers. Because lots of people use Blogger templates, the designs have prolif-erated throughout the web. They are arguably an improvement from the bland web log tem-plates previously available through services like LiveJournal.

Blogger templates may be further customized by bloggers, but the templates look so darned nice straight off the shelf that bloggers rarely bother to modify them. This results in thousands of "personal" web pages that look identical to each other.

At MySpace, on the other hand, each per-son's web page looks dizzyingly unique. The underlying layout structure at MySpace is the same for all pages, but surface-level design personalization is encouraged, evidenced by the fact that quality design templates are not provided. MySpace users are encouraged and empowered to design their own personal visual space.

Of course, users may choose to apply any number of prefabricated, hobbyist-designed templates to their page (available from sites like the aptly-named pimp-my-profile.com), but most of these templates are still far from pro-fessional (**Figure 6.4**).

Figure 6.3 A Rounders Blogger template, designed by Doug Bowman

Figure 6.4 "Twinkling of hot pink hearts" MySpace template, designed by bnbthatsme for pimp-my-profile.com

FORGET WHAT MODERNIST ARCHITECT LUDWIG MIES VAN DER ROHE SAID ABOUT "LESS IS MORE."

REMEMBER WHAT POSTMODERN ARCHITECT ROBERT VENTURI SAID: "LESS IS A BORE."

Customizing your Blogger site is like choosing between stock factory options when purchasing a new Volkswagen. Customizing your MySpace page is like taking your 1976 Impala into Bubba's Custom Body Shop for a facelift.

The former approach is safe, approved, and well designed. You are allowed a bit of personalization within the parameters of the Volkswagen brand.

The latter approach is something far more dangerous. You may wind up with an Impala that scrapes the ground at every speed bump and is refused entrance to the Country Club parking lot, but it will be undeniably your own. The MySpace Impala approach is also known as 1996 Dirt style.

Hobbyist web publishers whose "art" lies primarily in the content of their blog will choose Blogger over MySpace every time. And well they should. Why distract your readers with a visual design that makes your content semi-illegible? Simply choose a clean Blogger template and get on with your prose.

Hobbyist web publishers whose "art" is primarily in their blog design will hand-code their blog from scratch. But anyone hand-coding an RSS-enabled web log from scratch these days is probably a professional designer. So back to reality. Most contemporary hobbyists who want to express their personality via web design rather than web log prose will choose MySpace.

Both Blogger and MySpace are practically unbreakable, but for entirely different reasons. Hobbyists can't mess up their Blogger pages because the starter templates remain good-looking even after modification. Hobbyists can't mess up their MySpace pages because everyone's page looks like a train-wreck to begin with. Bad design acts as a kind of intentional affordance, a visual cue that suggests how something should be used. In this case, bad design suggests free play and invites reckless experimentation. You don't have to worry about wrecking a train that's already wrecked.

Increased Hobbyist Control

The goal of professional 1996 Dirt-style designers is not to use MySpace to display their own online design portfolios (that would be scary), but to create meta-design services like MySpace that encourage and support hobbyist customization and playfulness. There are two basic ways to increase hobbyists' control over the way something looks: You can increase their control over the visual design of the site; or you can allow them to modify, remix, and upload prepared source media. Let's take a look at both approaches.

PRIORITIZING HOBBYIST CONTROL OVER VISUAL DESIGN (OVERDESIGN)

Professional Dirt-style designers are meta-designers don't design a finished, overdetermined, static product. Instead, they design an intentionally broad field and invite the hobbyist designer to play in that field. Finding the right balance between an overdetermined system and an underdetermined system is the art of professional 1996 Dirt-style design.

You need to afford amateur designers enough control to engross them in the site-customization process, but not so much control that they can render the site inoperable. The key is to keep the essential functions of the site uncustomizable, while opening up the visual elements of the site to hobbyist customization. If you give hobbyists enough design rope to hang themselves, they eventually will. Professional Dirt-style designers are not ethically obliged to keep bad design from happening. On the contrary, they are ethically obliged to empower bad design. Don't save hobbyists from themselves. Deliver them to themselves (wrapped in blingy pink ribbon).

Professional 1996 Dirt-style designers give the people what they want and then some. Two good rules of thumb? Don't give them what you think they need. And don't give them what *you* think they want. Let *them* choose what they want. Sites like pimp-my-profile. com and blingee.com allow hobbyists to vote on prefabricated templates and animated .gifs. Hobbyists can then sort by popularity to see what other hobbyists like best. If what rises to the top seems like the bottom of the barrel to you, it may have something to do with the fact that not everyone in the world is a professional graphic designer.

Don't be surprised when your hobbyists' sites wind up overblown, overcrowded, and overdesigned. Go out of your way to allow this to happen. Forget what modernist architect Ludwig Mies van der Rohe said about "Less is more." Remember what postmodern architect Robert Venturi said: "Less is a bore." Dirt-style philosophy says you can never have too much of a good thing, and bling is always a good

thing. As a matter of fact, it don't mean a thing if it ain't got that bling!

PRIORITIZING HOBBYIST CONTROL OVER MEDIA CONTENT

Beyond hobbyist-customizable web pages, The 1996 Dirt-style approach can be applied to other online media. Any online community can be invited and empowered to remix songs, design CD cover art, create music videos, and modify other digital source materials. The results won't necessarily look like 1996 Dirt-style web design (since these media are not technically web sites), but the results will represent a hobbyist visual approach to these particular media.

Let's take a look at some examples.

Beck's The Information CD cover at amazon. com. Beck released his CD *The Information* with a blank cover and a set of stickers included in the liner notes. Four different sticker sets were distributed. People who purchased the CD were implicitly invited to design the CD's cover using the stickers, and they did (**Figure 6.5**).

For awhile now, Amazon shoppers have been invited to upload their own scanned or digitally photographed images of CD covers, which has traditionally been a fairly useless feature, since one person's scan of a CD cover is about the same as the next person's. However, the Beck CD covers have been different. Each scan is of a completely different cover. By combining offline hobbyist-customization with online hobbyist-participation, the amazon.com page for Beck's CD has been transformed into an interactive gallery of hobbyist design enthusiasts. Instant viral marketing. The last time I checked, there were 57 different customer images.

This is a perfect example of 1996 Dirt-style philosophy applied to print media content. The meta-designer (the person who created the stickers) controls the general parameters of the visual look. The hobbyists are not creating their own stickers. In this case, the stickers look like the kind of art teenagers would doodle on their trapper-keeper notebooks during English class in order to customize it. Once the basic visual parameters are established, the hobbyist is invited to play within this prescribed visual field. The meta-designer implicitly challenges the hobbyist: How customized can you make this CD cover by simply selecting, omitting, and collaging a limited set of stickers? How well can you express your own personality within this limited field of play?

Online at Amazon, this challenge leads to a multiuser game of hobbyist design skill and humor. All the while, the album's brand is being constructed by the very consumers who constitute its market. The brand of the album is not a static, corporate-generated image; it is an emerging, ongoing, hobbyist interactive event. Who owns the copyright to the hobbyist-generated CD cover images? The sticker designer, the record company, the hobbyists who stuck the stickers, or Amazon? The point is irrelevant, because the CD cover isn't the product. The music is the product. The CD cover is merely a designed marketing vehicle for selling the product.

This marketing strategy is very innovative, but it is hardly high-tech. Stickers have been

around for decades, and Amazon's "share your own customer images" feature has been around for years. It is the ingenious combination of these two previously existing technologies with an eye toward inviting customer participation that makes this particular application of the 1996 Dirt-style approach so successful.

David Byrne and Brian Eno audio at bush-of-ghosts.com. bush-of-ghosts.com promotes the re-issue of the Brian Eno and David Byrne seminal album, *My Life in the Bush of Ghosts*. Since the album is largely about sampling, remixing, and recontextualizing found audio material, a section of the site invites hobbyists to download the master audio tracks of two separate songs from the album. Under a creative commons license, hobbyists can remix these tracks however they like. Remixes can then be uploaded to the site and voted on by visitors. The last time I checked, 272 remixes had been submitted from all over the world.

By making these master audio tracks downloadable as individual .mp3 or .wav files, Eno and Byrne take what was a two-channel stereo song and open it up into a transparent, 24-track, remixable event. DJs visit the site not only to try their hand at remixing their heroes, but also to simply gain insight into the original mixing process of the album. bush-of-ghosts.com/remix transforms an album into an experimental audio clinic and community. Although the

Figure 6.5 Hobbyist-generated CD covers of Beck's *The Information*

site itself doesn't look at all like 1996 Dirt style, its approach to hobbyist-created audio is commendably Dirty.

Bjork, Nine Inch Nails, and Radiohead videos on YouTube. The popularity of YouTube has led to band-sponsored, hobbyist-generated video contests. The specific guidelines vary, but generally a band will put source material online (at least the audio of the song, often accompanied by video or photographic source material), and then the fans download the source material, create their own videos, and upload them to YouTube. Finally, winners are declared, and the winning work somehow winds up in an official band video. Bjork, Nine Inch Nails, and Radiohead are some of the more famous musicians who have held such contests.

Like album covers, the point of music videos is to market music to the fans; so why not simply let the fans make the videos? Record companies no longer have to do marketing research to determine which video approach fans like the best. The fans simply rate the videos on YouTube. The video with the highest rating is the one they liked the best. For every video that wins, dozens of other losing videos wind up flooding YouTube, virally promoting the same single. The contest gets press, the fans get involved, and the single gets promoted.

It all sounds very crass and commercial, but the same online social networking tools and open source Dirt-style philosophy can be used by artists to creatively collaborate with their fans. For example, Nine Inch Nails composed and recorded some experimental soundtrack music to a film that didn't exist, and then asked online fans to create visuals to accompany the music. Theoretically, these visuals will be viewed by the band to spur further creative audio output. The final collaborative result won't simply be a single promotional music video; it will look more like an online film festival. Whatever the final form of such hobbyist-created media experiments, the band and the music always wind up getting promoted.

As with 1996 Dirt-style web design, the art of 1996 Dirt-style media design is in finding the right balance between professional and hobbyist designer input. Will the fan-generated YouTube videos be mere prototypes for a future video that the band will ultimately pay a professional to create? Will several winning videos be used as actual source material and recollaged later by a professional? Will the winning hobbyist director receive award money to reshoot the video in a more professional manner? Will several winning videos be selected "as is" and used to create a compilation DVD for the

IT ALL SOUNDS VERY CRASS AND COMMERCIAL, BUT THE SAME ONLINE SOCIAL NETWORKING TOOLS AND OPEN SOURCE DIRT-STYLE PHILOSOPHY CAN BE USED BY ARTISTS TO CREATIVELY COLLABORATE WITH THEIR FANS.

band? How much visual source material will be offered to the fans? How strictly will they be required to incorporate it? Your structuring of the contest rules is just as much a part of your design process as the visual look of the source material you provide.

Modularization and Syndication

Contemporary 1996 Dirt-style sites like MySpace are modular. There is no cohesive, underlying grid system that visually unites and harmonizes the various components of a page. Modular sections of the page are simply cobbled together.

Modular design may not look great, but it suggests and enables syndication. Instead of hobbyists thinking of their web page as a single monolithic unit, they now think of it as a series of discrete components—individual blog posts added, and individual image files uploaded. All social networking sites come with built-in, off-the-shelf, syndication capabilities. Every blog post is potentially rebloggable via RSS technology.

When I subscribe to your blog and view your latest blog entry in my RSS newsreader software, or when I reblog your entry to my own group web log page, the original layout of your post disappears. All I see is the text, styled according to my own specifications. You lose control of the context in which your syndicated content appears, but you (potentially) gain an increased audience via viral distribution. One

way to embed your design intentions into your syndicated blog posts is by posting a digital image of your intended design. My CSS layout specifications can't override your .gif design.

Modular, syndicatable content gradually leads web log owners to care less about what any single blog page looks like and more about how those individual, syndicatable posts are received. They are no longer just designing for visitors to their blog; they are preparing content for syndication in any number of unforeseen contexts. When the syndicated content happens to be text, then the emphasis shifts from setting type to writing copy. When the syndicated content happens to be visual (.jpg images, YouTube videos, and yes, even animated .gifs), the emphasis shifts from web page design to static print or animation design. Thus modular design and syndication gradually lead hobbyist web publishers away from web page design per se and more toward other forms of media design.

Modularization and syndication can lead to a kind of blurb, tweet (burp, belch) online sound-byte culture. Site design is no longer considered holistically. No post (or thought) is over two paragraphs long. Whether or not such a culture should be actively resisted by professional web designers is an ethical question worth serious consideration. Whatever you decide, online media currently tend toward modularization and syndication. They are part and parcel of the contemporary, hobbyist-generated, Dirt-style web-design landscape.

Glittery GIF Animations,
Outer Space, Tron

Three hallmarks of 1996 Dirt style are glittery animated .gifs, tiling backgrounds of stars in outer space, and anything that looks like it came from the 1982 movie *Tron*.

Blingee.com and sites like it allow users to add reams of ridiculous, gratuitous glitter

animation to any image for free (**Figure 6.6**). The newly blinged-out image is saved as an animated .gif, ready to be displayed on any MySpace page. In 1996, you had to have serious cell animation skills to achieve such intensely wacky tackiness. Now all it takes is a spare five minutes. We've come a long a way.

Blingee.com lets you add anything from rainbows and tiaras to crossbones and marijuana leaves. It appeals equally to wanna-be gangster rappers and cuddly kitten owners. It gives the people what they want: bling.

Starry backgrounds are a staple of 1996 Dirt style because the interweb is also known as cyber*space*, And space is made of stars. Unfortunately, space is also made up of blackness, which makes many Dirt-style sites very dark. To add insult to injury, Dirt-style typography cannot simply be white. It must be some form of illegible neon green, invisible deep purple, or my favorite—blood red. Nothing says Dirt style like maroon text on a black background.

Finally, in keeping with all things retro, the most recent slew of Dirt-style enthusiasts advocate a kind of 1980s New Wave neon look, similar to the computer-generated sets of *Tron*. Art deco-esque patterns of neon blues and reds are combined with glitchy data compression errors to produce an oddball retro-geekiness that only a contemporary Dirt-style fetishist could love. This approach actually looks pretty cool ... to anyone who thinks the special effects for the 1980 roller disco musical *Xanadu* are cool.

Background Killer: Horror Vacui

Horror vacui is a fear of blank spaces. It is characteristic of certain outsider art made by mental patients. People with horror vacui have no psychological peace until every last inch of blank space on a page is filled with patterns. 1996 Dirt style takes the same approach to web pages. Dirt-style designers kill their negative background space with tiling background images—preferably sparkly animated .gifs.

It would be too distracting to put your text directly on top of these blinged-out, tiling background animations. On the other hand, it would be a shame to hide your *beautiful* background pattern beneath an opaque white color. This is why Dirt-style designers often place their body text on top of a solidly colored, semi-translucent .png image. That way the blinged-out background of the overall page is still slightly visible through the .png. This technique renders the body text only slightly illegible. Problem solved! MySpace allows users to set these translucency levels without ever bothering with Photoshop or .pngs.[1]

Figure 6.6 a Blingee-enhanced self-portrait of the author

Uses

1996 Dirt style may seem idiosyncratic, anachronistic, and just plain bad, but it has several practical contemporary uses.

It is appropriate for an easy-to-use social-networking community like MySpace where hobbyists are encouraged to express themselves via visual design. The front page of the community site need not be designed in 1996 Dirt style (MySpace's front page is not), but the customization options that the hobbyists are given should allow them to wind up with their own version of 1996 Dirt style should they so desire.

1996 Dirt style is also appropriate for any corporately owned online service that wants to come across as easy to use and nonthreatening. Google's logo is a great example of how subtle Dirt-style design can increase a site's perceived approachability. The Google logo was designed by Ruth Kedar in 1999, and it hasn't been redesigned since. Why? Because it suggests a kind of no-brainer, any-kid-can-use-it functionality. Even the cheesy drop-shadow alludes to an earlier hobbyist web.

Along the same lines, Dirt-style design is appropriate for any homemade, non-corporate service that wants to come across as personal. A bed and breakfast is a good example. According to internet theorist Olia Lialina, "When you see a site made by the hotel owner, where she writes about her hobbies as well as the hotel facilities and also makes a portrait gallery of local cats and dogs, you think about the high level of personal service at this hotel."[2] 1996 Dirt-style design is a way of showing that

an actual human being is responsible for a particular web enterprise.

However you decide to use 1996 Dirt style, don't use it purposelessly, or it will simply look like you are a bad designer. Use it for a reason that fits the goals of the site that you (or your hobbyists) are building.

● ● ●

As interactive designers, we have an ethical obligation to design things well. To cite an extreme example, a clear interactive interface is essential for the control panels of a nuclear power plant. Anything less would be unethical, irresponsible, and dangerous. But MySpace is not a nuclear power plant. If MySpace hobbyists want to waste time online, vogue around, bling-out, and generally pile design atrocity upon design atrocity, there will be no nuclear meltdown. I propose that there are times when good design involves facilitating hobbyists' own blissful, ridiculous, gaudy, over-indulgence. When you are called upon as a professional meta-designer to facilitate such overindulgence don't forget to bring the bling.

IN THAT EMPIRE, THE CRAFT OF CARTOGRAPHY

ATTAINED SUCH PERFECTION THAT THE MAP

OF A SINGLE PROVINCE COVERED THE SPACE

OF AN ENTIRE CITY, AND THE MAP OF THE

EMPIRE ITSELF AN ENTIRE PROVINCE. IN THE

COURSE OF TIME, THESE EXTENSIVE MAPS

WERE FOUND SOMEHOW WANTING, AND SO

THE COLLEGE OF CARTOGRAPHERS EVOLVED

A MAP OF THE EMPIRE THAT WAS OF THE SAME

SCALE AS THE EMPIRE AND THAT COINCIDED

WITH IT POINT FOR POINT.

— JORGE LUIS BORGES AND ADOLFO BIOY CASARES

07 | *CORKBOARD SPRAWL STYLE*

Since the beginning of the web, web "pages" have been thought of as printed pages. They are not called web screens, web scrolls, web spaces, web maps, or any number of other things that they could just as easily be called. HTML was originally created to help academics more readily share academic research "papers" with each other, so it made sense to think of each screen of browser content as a page from a longer, text-based paper.

But a web page is not really a page. It can conceivably have an infinite height and width. It can unfold and expand at the click of a button. It can even be zoomed into, revealing increasingly detailed layers of content. A web page can spread out like a physical corkboard with individual posted messages, or fold in on itself like origami. Once you are willing to embrace a bit of scrolling and folding, all sorts of new, post-page spatial analogies begin to emerge.

Technically, the page analogy is inaccurate for the web. A printed page is always read at the same scale, regardless of who is reading it. *The New York Times* is read every morning by millions of people—tall, short, fat, and thin—but the dimensions of the newspaper itself never change. In digital space, however, the scale of a web page varies depending on the screen resolution of the monitor displaying it. Browser text can be enlarged or shrunk at the click of a button. A web page has no fixed height or width. Finally, a printed magazine page is taller than it is wide (portrait format), whereas a computer monitor is wider than it is tall (landscape format). All of these differences suggest that the page analogy is ripe to be replaced by more experimental models.

Corkboard Sprawl style treats a web page as something other than a printed page of text. Corkboard Sprawl designers are like experimental mapmakers, pushing the boundaries of what a single web page can contain.

Influences

Other than the printed text page, which surfaces found in the physical world contain textual information? Before the radical page-by-page design of the book, scrolls contained textual information. Indeed, the browser scrollbar is influenced by the technology of the printed scroll. Billboards, posters, and movie theater marquees all contain textual information. They also take up a lot of space in the physical world. Since visible screen space is always limited, Corkboard Sprawl style is influenced by two real-world surface technologies that are capable of fitting a lot of information into a relatively small space—cork bulletin boards and origami.

Analog Corkboards

Real-world cork bulletin boards (not to be confused with their online Bulletin Board System counterparts) allow people to post printed messages in public spaces. These messages are printed on paper of various shapes and sizes. The typography of each message is different.

Corkboards are chronological collages made up of miniature posters, with the most recent ones on top. Even if the posters overlap, you can

CORKBOARD SPRAWL DESIGNERS ARE LIKE EXPERIMENTAL MAPMAKERS,

PUSHING THE BOUNDARIES OF WHAT A SINGLE WEB PAGE CAN CONTAIN.

always physically move the top posters to reveal the bottom ones. The borders of the corkboard are not rigidly enforced; often posters hang over the edges. Limited horizontal and vertical space is overcome by stacking things on top of each other in dimensional "z-axis" space. All of these characteristics influence the Corkboard Sprawl style of web design.

Origami

Origami, the Japanese art of paper folding, has become quite advanced and complex in recent years with the help of mathematics, computers, and innovative origami artists like Robert J. Lang. A single page of paper can be folded to make an infinite number of intricate objects. Corkboard Sprawl designers fold and unfold digital "paper" using transitional animations. Nothing is actually folded, but it appears that sections of the site are decompressing and recompressing as the user surfs. Rather than metaphorically flipping through pages of a book, the visitor is metaphorically unfolding and contracting what seems to be a single plane of malleable space.

Characteristics

Corkboard Sprawl style intentionally undermines the metaphor of page and book. A Corkboard Sprawl site is not a book made up of discrete pages. It's not even a screen of fixed dimensions framed by the browser. Instead, it is a sprawling, rambling, morphing, telescoping, holistic space navigated by the user. *Surfing* once again becomes a useful descriptive term. Users are no longer "flipping" through pages of a book; they are sorting, sifting, exploring, drifting, and surfing through the "page" of the site.

Corkboard Sprawl sites are not unified by a predetermined, harmonizing, underlying grid. Instead, each screen seems to have come together piecemeal, without forethought, as if components were added chronologically as they arrived. This is often not the case, but the sites are purposefully designed to feel this way. Corkboard Sprawl sites are either layered or folded (or both); there is always some hidden content beneath the surface or around the bend.

Corkboard Sprawl style can have a worn, analog texture (like decomposing advertisements on bulletin boards), but not all sites take the corkboard metaphor so literally. Some Corkboard Sprawl sites use clean vector animations and actually look very digital. It is their underlying architecture and their approach to the screen "page" that make them Corkboard Sprawl-esque.

Unbounded Layout

Corkboard Sprawl sites need not be bound by the edges of the browser. As long as you are willing to allow for vertical and horizontal scrolling, visitors can scroll through a much larger content area. The trick is to build the site so that scrolling is invited. This means that all of the content areas must overlap and lead off the edge of the browser. If you leave gaps between content areas, then users may think they have come to the end of your sprawl, and never scroll to see what lies beyond.

According to the logic of the printed page, vertical scrolling on the web is allowable; but only in small amounts, since nobody wants to perpetually unfold a newspaper. According to the logic of the printed page, your most important content should appear "above the fold" (immediately on the screen prior to any vertical scrolling). No article should be more than two screens long. If it needs to be longer, you must divide the long article into a multipage article, providing links from one page to the next.

According to the logic of the printed page, horizontal scrolling is strongly discouraged, because nobody wants to scroll back and forth across a screen to read a single line of text. Horizontal scrolling is only tolerated if your page is built in columns so that the horizontal scrolling reveals a full, undivided, extra right column.

But what if your front page is not an online newspaper? What if there are no full columns of text? What if your page is simply a compendium of images, links, and short explanatory blurbs? Then vertical and horizontal scrolling are perfectly appropriate, provided you give your user enough visual cues to expect such behavior.

constantvzw.org is a good example of unbounded Corkboard Sprawl layout in conjunction with vertical scrolling (**Figure 7.1**). Constant is a Brussels-based media arts organization focused on collaboration across networks. It hosts performance events, conferences, and tutorials.

The background of Constant's main page is filled with overlapping thumbnail images taken at these events. Refreshing the page loads a different set of images every time. Scattered among the images are randomly generated keywords that apply to the site. Clicking on one of them initiates a search for that word on the site. Clicking on a thumbnail image leads to an enlarged version of that image in a Flickr-like database.

The Constant navigation always floats above the images, so usability is not hindered by this Corkboard background approach. The thumbnail images aren't simply visual filler; they actually lead to larger pages that describe the images and place them next to related images. By featuring these thumbnails on its front page, the organization shows that it values the individuals who participate in Constant-sponsored events. By collaging and intermingling thumbnail images from different events, Constant shows that it values collaboration and the cross-pollination of ideas. The unbounded layout of the front page reveals the core values of the organization.

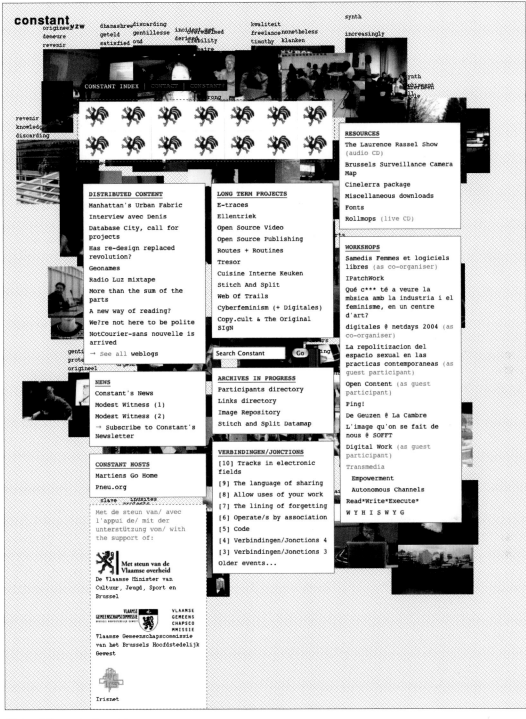

Figure 7.1 constantvzw.org

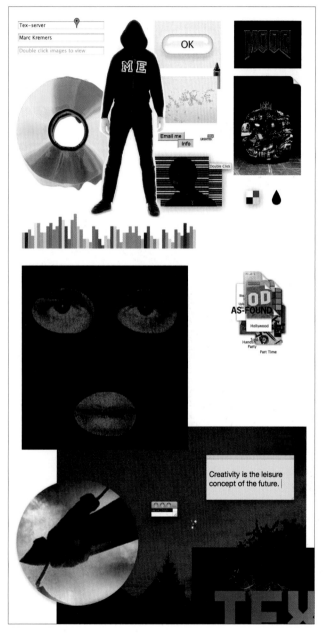

Figure 7.2 tex-server.org

tex-server.org (version 5) is a fun example of unbounded vertical layout (**Figure 7.2**). Tex-Server is the experimental online portfolio of Marc Kremers. The interface of the site itself is an ongoing exploration in cryptic navigation design. Currently, tex-server.org is a long link list to Kremer's various art projects. Each image on the page is a link. Some images are animated; some overlap; all sprawl downward.

The layout of tex-server.org invites user exploration and participation. It is not merely the usual link list of text descriptions. It is not even the semi-usual link list of rectangular screenshots from each project. Instead, each image occupies a unique space and form on the page. Will visitors click the largest image first, the brightest image first, the most animated image first, or the topmost image first? Does the topmost image lead to the most recent work? Is the largest image the most important? Are the images simply randomly placed as Kremers adds new work to the site? Kremers uses this unbounded layout to develop his own idiosyncratic hierarchy of meaning.

billyharveymusic.com uses Flash, masking tape, and Polaroid pictures to create a sprawling layout without using the scrollbar (**Figure 7.3**). Clicking on any single Polaroid picture zooms in on it (**Figure 7.4**). The site promotes slacker singer-songwriter Billy Harvey. As you click through the different Polaroids of what are presumably different rooms in Billy's house, his animated likeness pursues you from photo to photo, perpetually welcoming you to the site as if it were his home. Although the site is technically sophisticated, its casual, almost haphazard

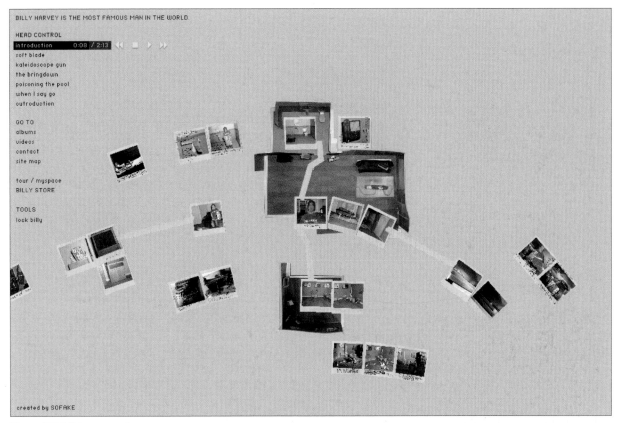

Figure 7.3 billyharveymusic.com
from far away

Figure 7.4 billyharveymusic.com up close

‹ Borders of Paradise
A promotional poster for Big Theater's production of Borders of Paradise, directed by Ellie Heyman. A blue watercolor wash with handwritten text.

‹ Concert Poster: Mahjongg
A promotional poster for the Empty Bottle. Halftone vinyl film gives the illusion of movement or modulation as you

Figure 7.5 pluralplural.com

layout makes it seem as if the musician simply cobbled together a virtual version of his own real world living space.

The online portfolio of the design firm Plural is laid out on a clean modernist grid (**Figure 7.5**), but the entire site is actually a single "page" in Flash. Clicking on any link slides the cursor directly to a target location on that page (**Figure 7.6**). Only the left menu remains in place. The sliding is not just vertical and horizontal. If the quickest path to the target location is diagonal, then the entire page slides diagonally. There are no browser scrollbars, and no zooming in and out. The user simply shuffles

and slides around the same large page instead of flipping through a series of separate, smaller pages. Once you get used to the functionality, this form of navigation is surprisingly economical and sensible.

User-Modifiable Layout

Like real-world corkboards, some Corkboard Sprawl pages allow users to rearrange various pieces of content. User-customizable layouts are nothing new. iGoogle allows users to customize the location of their news widgets by dragging and dropping them to new locations on the

and Killer Whales. Bold typography and color are used to describe their "NEW MUSIC."

blue watercolor wash

pl.

plural

about
contact
clients
blog
awards
links
store
work
  posters
  Cluster
  Musical Architecture
  Morton Feldman
  books
  web
  identities
  motion
  packaging
  experimentation
  Interpretations Magnetic Tape
  Visualizing Soundscapes
  Visual Timbre
  There was a Stone
  Chaos
  type

The Seventies - 70/1801
about growing up in the seventies. The cover and box set on that time. Limited Edition Letter Pressed Book.

‹ Here Then There

Mapping explorations based on the question: "How can we visually describe the directions from place A to B in a city?" Created in Michael Renner's Inquiry by D Workshop. Basel School of Design. 2007.

Figure 7.6 pluralplural.com during a transitional slide

page. But the end result at iGoogle is always tight and gridded. You are only allowed to place the content in certain perfectly aligned locations. User-modifiable Corkboard Sprawl layouts allow users to place the content anywhere they like.

The website for the Art Gallery of Knoxville is one such sprawling site that allows the user to move content anywhere (**Figure 7.7**). Indeed, the user must move certain pieces of content to reveal hidden content underneath. The individual pieces of content look less like corkboard flyers and more like Post-it notes. Clicking on any piece of content brings it into sharper focus. When you are finished reading the Post-it notes and are looking at the movable images, you can stack them in a corner out of the way as you dig through the rest of the content. In true corkboard fashion, the site scrolls both horizontally and vertically.

This kind of interactive layout requires user investigation. It also intentionally defies an imposed structural hierarchy. For an art gallery that encourages collaborative participation and features work that is perpetually in progress, this design approach is ideal.

Figure 7.7 theartgalleryofknoxville.com

Unfolding Layout (Spatial Flash)

Some Corkboard Sprawl sites unfold as the user surfs them, reverse origami style. All of these sites use Flash technology. Technically, the sites simply move across a Flash timeline from target frame to target frame. It is the interstitial animations between static states that make the sites seem like they are unfolding (or expanding, or exploding, or evolving).

Originally, Flash was a tool for creating non-interactive vector animations. I call this kind of Flash *Splash Flash*, because it is often used to create obtrusively long splash page animations prior to any actual site content. Later Flash was used to create entire interactive sites that behaved very much like regular HTML sites. I call this second kind of Flash *Site Flash*.

Savvy designers combined the two types of Flash to create a hybrid animal that I call *Spatial Flash*. Spatial Flash is both interactive and animated. The animations come in between the interactive states. They make the site seem to unfold. Each click triggers a new animation that leads to a new interactive state with different choices. Your submenu options emerge as you surf.

Navigating this kind of spring-loaded layout feels less like turning pages and more like unfolding a piece of paper, or zooming in and out of a landscape, or hatching the egg of a giant lizard, or whatever metaphor the designer chooses to invoke.

leoburnett.ca (the online portfolio of the Canadian branch of the Leo Burnett advertising company) uses a simple pencil and paper metaphor for its navigation. At first the user

sees the Leo Burnett signature and a black pencil (**Figure 7.8**). Rolling over the pencil explodes the signature and reveals several top-level links (**Figure 7.9**). The pencil then follows the user's mouse, making drawing marks on the digital paper. Clicking on a link zooms into that particular section, revealing its submenu links (**Figure 7.10**). Rolling over a submenu link further zooms, revealing a thumbnail image of the link's content (**Figure 7.11**). To go back to the top level, you simply click on any blank space.

leoburnett.ca sets us up to expect the same old page metaphor, and then surprises us with a telescoping, unfolding Corkboard Sprawl

Background Killer: The Content Itself

Corkboard Sprawl sites are either unbounded by the borders of the browser or they unfold and cover the full screen. In either case, there is no real background other than the content itself. Since users already have to scroll vertically and horizontally, they simply scroll to the edge of the content, at which point the page ends and no background is necessary.

In the case of unfolding Flash layouts, the background gradually fills up with content as a user surfs the site. The background is left as negative space until it gets filled with content.

If the unfolding Flash animation you've designed is not large enough to fill the entire screen, simply invoke a popup window the size of the Flash animation. That way your unfolding animation covers the entire popup window without having to cover the entire screen.

layout. All of this innovative visual navigation is accompanied by ambient audio of the pencil drawing and playful "zooming" sounds as we click deeper into the site.

We Fail (the design duo of Jordan Stone and Martin Hughes) are masters of using Flash to create novel spatial metaphors of telescoping and unfolding. (Jordan Stone also designed the Billy Harvey site above.) One of my favorite examples of their commercial design is a promotional site they did for ESPN's X Games, an annual event focusing on extreme action sports.

The four sections of the site radiate out from the four corners of a central X. Each section focuses on a single athlete from a different extreme sport. All the sections are unique to that athlete's personality. The sections unfold one at a time as the user clicks on different edges of the X (**Figure 7.12**). Only when all four sections are unfolded is the screen completely filled (**Figure 7.13**). Clicking on a section zooms into that section, revealing submenu options and animated videos of the athletes welcoming you and telling you that their section is the best (**Figure 7.14**).

The site unfolds with extreme chaotic animations. Even after it has unfolded, elements in each section continue to move. The whole site seems to breathe with a life of its own. These expressive animations combine with a playful, idiosyncratic illustration style to give this site character and energy. It effectively supplements the ESPN extreme sports television broadcasts by providing a novel and engaging backstory appropriate to the alternative athletes it promotes.

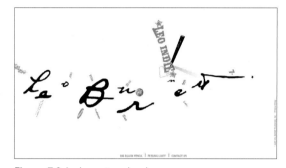

Figure 7.8 leoburnett.ca welcome

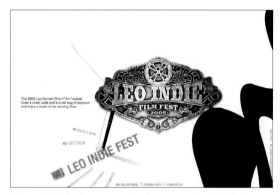

Figure 7.9 leoburnett.ca level one

Figure 7.10 leoburnett.ca level two

Figure 7.11 leoburnett.ca level three

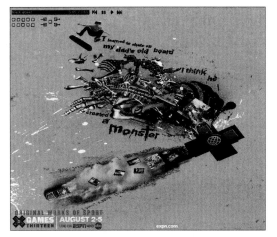

Figure 7.12 wefail.com/xgames/
with two sections unfolded

Figure 7.13 wefail.com/xgames/ with four sections unfolded

Figure 7.14 wefail.com/xgames/ section detail

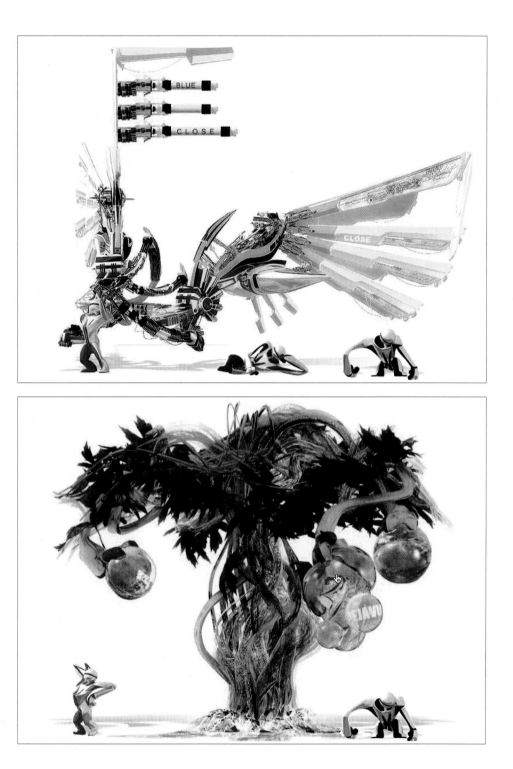

Figure 7.15 xiiin.com/
idol_ani.asp blue section

Figure 7.16 xiiin.com/
idol_ani.asp red section

Figure 7.17 xiiin.com/idol_ani.asp black section

Origami layouts can be a way of showcasing character animation. XIIIN is a South Korean marketing company specializing in animated characters. Part of its site features three characters: blue, red, and black robots. Clicking on the blue robot causes its chest to open, revealing a complex, motorized, winged machine containing the submenu links for that section (**Figure 7.15**). Clicking on the red robot causes it to transform into a translucent red tree (**Figure 7.16**). The submenu links for that section are the fruit of the tree. Clicking on the black robot hatches a giant green lizard with submenu links dripping from its tongue (**Figure 7.17**). The transitional animations provide a narrative connection between the tiny robots and their expanded states. xiiin.com proves that unfolding layouts can assume practically any form.

If the XIIIN animations are strange, the animations at tokyoplastic.com, an experimental animation firm, are downright surreal. A tiny girl is swallowed by a large black tree with Venus Fly Trap blossoms acting as links (**Figure 7.18**). The rest of the morphing animations are so complex and unexpected, to capture them as a series of static screenshots would fail to do them justice. Japanese flags turn into mechanical mouths. White squares turn into two-legged hopping, swimming cubes. The border of the content area is constantly redrawn. Trap doors

Uses

open at the bottom of the screen, occasionally swallowing the site's content. We are set up to expect one thing and then we are perpetually undermined by surprise after surprise.

It's almost as if this site has its own warped, mechanical mind, improvising these bizarre animations as it goes along. tokyoplastic.com is a masterfully scripted, paced, and choreographed example of Corkboard Sprawl unfolding.

Corkboard Sprawl style is useful for a rock band site, a concert venue site with regularly posted events, a frequently updated portfolio site, and any site regularly updated with small blurbs of content. The site for the British band The Good, The Bad, and The Queen incorporates a Corkboard Sprawl approach to display thumbnail images of recent press clippings (**Figure 7.19**). These images are piled on top of each other in bulletin board style. Each thumbnail launches a pop-up window with the full article in Flash Paper format.

Unfolding Corkboard Sprawl layouts are useful for entertainment branding sites that tell the backstory of a film or augment an offline media experience. These sites don't have to

Figure 7.18 tokyoplastic.com

tell the entire story of the film, album, or TV series. They only have to create an engaging online experience that supplements and promotes their offline media. Unfolding, animated layouts seem especially ideal for online promotion of offline video games, since gamers are already used to navigating interactive spaces that look less like book pages and more like emergent worlds.

Corkboard Sprawl style is *not* useful for conveying large columns of textual content. This does not make it an illegitimate design style. A style may be inapplicable to text-centric layout and still serve other useful functions on the commercial web. After all, not every site is cnn.com.

● ● ●

Historically, it is understandable why web design began with the metaphor of the printed page. It was a useful place to start, and it is still useful for sites with lots of text content.

Moving web design beyond the page metaphor is a little like the historic transition from radio to television. When advertisers first began working with television as a medium, they approached the commercials as if they were radio commercials. They would still say, "Friends, I'm standing next to this beautiful Maytag appliance," even though the television audience could plainly see the appliance. Eventually, they allowed for the fact that their new audience had eyes as well as ears.

Figure 7.19 thegoodthebadandthequeen.com

Likewise, we need not design web pages as if they were books pages simply because we still call them pages. If your page wants to sprawl, let it sprawl. If it wants to unfold, let it unfold. If it wants to explode, invert, contort, cavort, hatch, careen, congeal … well, you get the idea!

COME, COME, COME INTO
MY WORLD

—KYLIE MINOGUE

08 | *FULLSCREEN FASHION STYLE*

There was a time when Internet bandwidth could not support high-resolution media, but that time has passed. If you are a photographer or even a filmmaker with an online portfolio, you can assume your potential clients have the bandwidth to view your high-resolution images and video clips.

If the main content of your site is high-resolution visual media (such as photography, video, or animation), it makes sense to assign more screen real estate to your visuals than to your text. Gone are the days when the browser displays a page of text with an occasional illustrative image. The browser has become a window frame into a lush, sensory, visual world.

Fullscreen Fashion style treats the browser as a window frame and seeks to fill it with as much visual impact as possible. This often means filling the entire window with visual content. Text is still used for navigational and explanatory purposes, but it is no longer the site's primary content. Fullscreen Fashion sites often feel less like standard web sites and more like slide shows, films, immersive game environments, or surreal worlds.

Influences

Fullscreen Fashion sites that feature photography have been primarily influenced by glossy glamour magazines with full page, full-bleed photographs. Fullscreen Fashion sites that feature animated Flash environments have usually been influenced by surrealist painters. In the former case, the screen is filled to showcase as much photography as possible. In the latter case, it is filled to create a standalone, surreal world, unframed by the context of browser buttons and standard interface elements.

Glossy Glamour Magazines

Full-bleed printing is printing beyond the border of the visible page. The oversized page is then cropped so that the printed image ends at the very edge of the visible page. This kind of printing is commonplace for most magazine covers, but glamour and fashion magazines use this technique throughout, for everything from feature articles to advertisements. The close-up face of a model, for example, is particularly arresting when printed full-bleed. It is hyper-real, and larger than life. It seems intimate (or at least pleasurably voyeuristic). Glamour magazines use glossy finish rather than matte finish because it makes their photographs shiny, glistening, vivid, elegant, and sexy.

Fullscreen Fashion web designers employ the full-bleed technique by filling the entire browser window with imagery.

They achieve a kind of digital glossiness by using high-resolution images, prepared in Photoshop to achieve the maximum RGB color vividness possible.

Surrealism

Surrealist artists like René Magritte and Salvador Dali painted visually realistic but objectively impossible scenes. Their paintings have a certain internal logic: They make sense in and of themselves, but compared to waking reality, they are confounding and absurd. Fullscreen Fashion designers use Flash to create similarly surreal worlds, except theirs are animated and interactively navigable. The navigation is often cryptic and nonstandard, but it makes sense according to the surreal logic of these immersive environments.

THE GOAL OF A FULLSCREEN FASHION DESIGNER IS TO FILL THE MONITOR WITH IMAGERY WHENEVER POSSIBLE. FULLSCREEN IMAGERY IS THE DEFINING VISUAL CHARACTERISTIC OF THIS STYLE.

Characteristics

Fullscreen Fashion style is characterized by an emphasis on imagery over text. This emphasis influences every aspect of web design: layout, navigation, interaction, typographic treatment, and site architecture. Where do you put your text when the entire screen is taken up with imagery? How do you create meaningful navigation without text or icons? How many levels deep can a menuless site go before it requires a popup window? The answers to these questions determine the characteristics of Fullscreen Fashion style.

Fullscreen Photography

The goal of a Fullscreen Fashion designer is to fill the monitor with imagery whenever possible. Fullscreen imagery is the defining visual characteristic of this style.

The front page of the Creative Time website is a great example of arresting wall-to-wall imagery (**Figure 8.1**). The background image is always a photograph of the public artwork that the organization has recently commissioned. The image changes when you refresh the page.

Figure 8.1 creativetime.org

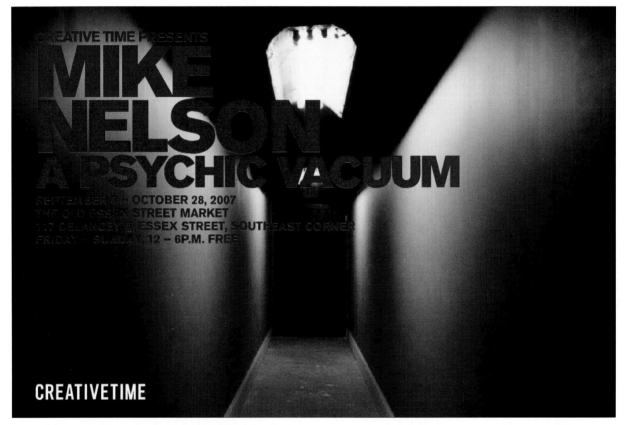

Figure 8.2 creativetime.org/programs/archive/2007/nelson/

Regardless of the background image content, it always fits with the bold sans-serif logo typography and the white navigation box containing black text. The logo is a .png with background transparency, so it seamlessly anti-aliases into whatever color happens to be beneath it.

Another section of the site features the same bold, industrial Helvetica type over a fullscreen photograph of a Mike Nelson installation (**Figure 8.2**). The effect is intentionally dramatic and subtly disturbing.

Technically, the Creative Time images are not really background images. They are simply inline images with other content stacked on top of them, using the z-axis stacking ability of CSS. The source background images themselves are 1000-pixels wide and roughly 750-pixels high (a 1.3 aspect ratio suitable to the proportions of most computer monitors). The width of the image is set in HTML to 100%, and the height of the image is not specified. This way, regardless of visitor's browser dimensions, the image will stretch to fill the width of the screen. Yet because no height is specified, the image will never distort its original proportions. In the worst-case scenario, there is a bit of extra negative space at the bottom of the screen.

These background images weigh around 100 KB to 200 KB. Their resolution is high enough to withstand a bit of browser enlarging without looking bad. And their weight is thin enough for them to download in a reasonable amount of time. The Creative Time site employs several technically simple but ingenious hacks to achieve a dramatic fullscreen effect.

White or Black Negative Space

Not all Fullscreen Fashion images make it to the browser's edge. In those instances when you choose to not fill the screen completely with an image, your negative space should be either white or black, depending on the effect you want to achieve. White brightens the work and makes it more approachable and playful. Black makes the work seem more mysterious and serious. Technically, black and white aren't colors, so they don't compete with the RGB colors of the actual photographic images.

The online portfolio of photographer Uwe Ditz uses a white background combined with red typography that is interspersed among red squares. Rolling over any square transforms it into a photographic thumbnail for several seconds, until it eventually fades back into a red square (**Figure 8.3**). Clicking on a square causes its full image to appear in a lightbox fashion, superimposed atop the faded background navigation (**Figure 8.4**). You can then navigate from image to image in this lightbox environment, or return at any time to the original navigation scheme. Once you visit a photograph, its square turns a lighter shade of red.

Ditz has a series of red-themed photographs, and his site design plays on that theme. The single-word description of each photographic series is concise but also whimsical and inviting. The serif typeface indicates elegance, while the bright red indicates humor. The site design matches the personality of the featured work.

Figure 8.3 uwe-ditz.com menu

Figure 8.4 uwe-ditz.com lightbox

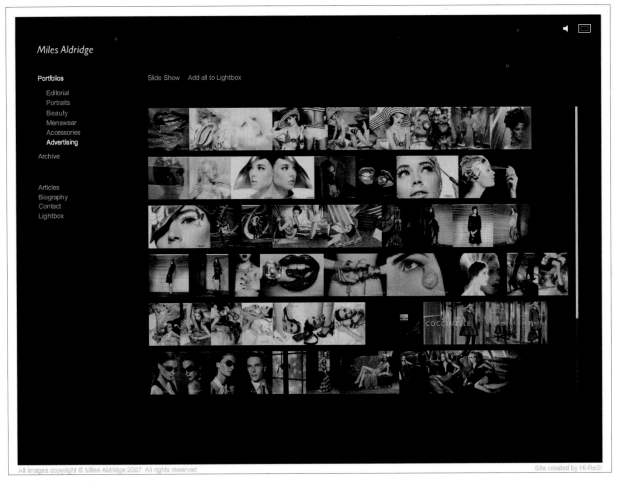

Figure 8.5 milesaldridge.com

The portfolio site of photographer Miles Aldridge is darker and more serious. It begins with a Flash splash page slide show of large images set against a black background. Clicking on any one of these images transforms the site into a fullscreen gallery of glossy, colorful thumbnail images (**Figure 8.5**). The browser toolbar disappears, replaced by a subtle white border, which is a more suitable frame for this glamorous content than the browser's default chrome.

The Doll
Numero
2007

Figure 8.6 milesaldridge.com

Clicking on any thumbnail image causes everything to fade out and a large version of the thumbnail to gradually fade in (**Figure 8.6**). Clicking on the large image reverses the process. While in large image mode, you can use unobtrusive arrows to navigate from image to image.

Because there is space for a menu to the left of the thumbnails, the site can be a second-level deep before having to resort to lightbox mode. This means future sections of additional thematic content can be added without having to radically redesign the site's architecture. A thin Flash scrollbar to the right of the site accommodates larger galleries that have more thumbnail images. From its thin sans-serif typography to its subtle transition fades, the design of milesaldridge.com suits the nature of its photographic content.

The Dolce & Gabbana site also uses a black background in conjunction with large, near-fullscreen images (**Figure 8.7**). The women's section is on the left, and the men's is on the right. A scrolling menu of thumbnail images appears beside the larger images, and a text menu appears beside that. The central space of the site is reserved for the large images.

As long as you are scrolling through the thumbnail menu, the text menu options disappear (except for the name of the section where you are). Moving your mouse onto the text menu area causes the text menu options to appear and the large central image to blur (**Figure 8.8**). There are actually two separate menu systems and a large content area accessible at any given time, but this fading trick keeps the overall site from seeming too cluttered. The text menu yields to the images when appropriate, and vice versa.

The edges of the Dolce & Gabbana runway photographs fade into the black background of the site. This makes the models seem as if they are emerging from a film noir scene, giving the entire site an air of mystery and intimacy. It also makes the colors of the garments dramatically lucid in contrast to the black background.

THERE ARE ACTUALLY TWO SEPARATE MENU SYSTEMS AND A LARGE CONTENT AREA ACCESSIBLE AT ANY GIVEN TIME, BUT THIS FADING TRICK KEEPS THE OVERALL SITE FROM SEEMING TOO CLUTTERED.

Figure 8.7 www.dolcegabbana.com/dg/

Figure 8.8 www.dolcegabbana.com/dg/

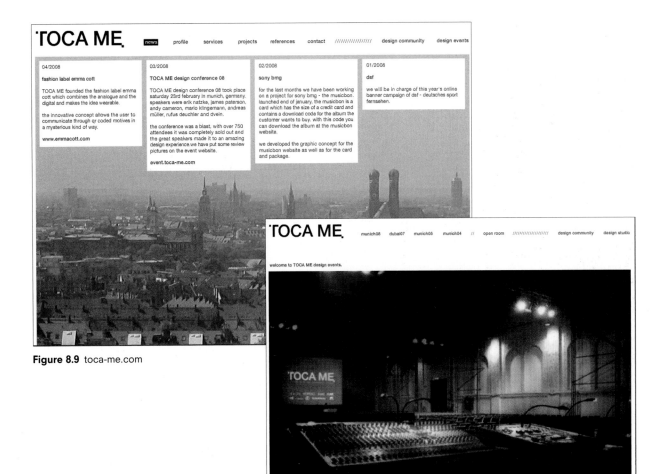

Figure 8.9 toca-me.com

Figure 8.10 toca-me.com

Unobtrusive Text

Once you have filled most of your screen with an image, where do you put the text? One solution is to reserve a menu section above or beside your main image content area, and put your text there (**Figure 8.9**). Another solution is to put the your text in a white (or black) box directly on top of the image (**Figure 8.10**). toca-me.com uses both solutions. On some pages, its images even recede a bit when you mouse over the menu area, revealing subordinate text. Like other sites in this chapter, toca-me.com gains extra screen space by using a splash page to launch its site in a new browser window that lacks a toolbar.

The white boxes on top of the cityscape image work because there is no important visual content in the sky for the boxes to cover. The site's designers selected this particular fullscreen image to synchronize with the layout of the text content.

Figure 8.11 smo-smo.com

Another solution to the text placement dilemma is to put the text directly on top of the fullscreen image. The challenge is to make the text legible while keeping it from detracting from the visual impact of the image.

smo-smo.com, the portfolio of designer Isabel Pettinato, solves this problem by placing bold sans-serif text on top of background images that are primarily meant to add visual texture (**Figure 8.11**).

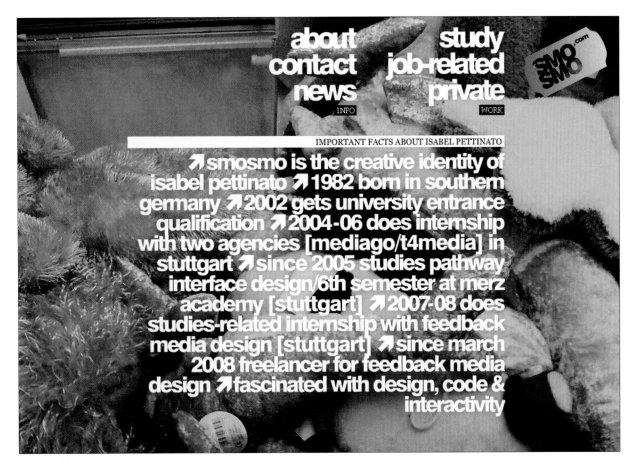

Figure 8.12 smo-smo.com

The background images slide across the screen in response to the movement of the cursor, causing the text to move in relation to the images. The background images also rotate regularly (**Figure 8.12**). None of this matters, because the images are always darker than the white text on top of them, and they never contain any single focal object to obscure. Like the Creative Time logo, the smo-smo.com text is bold enough to be visible without a solid content box behind it.

Shallow Site Depth

Fullscreen Fashion sites don't have a lot of screen space for menus and submenus, which means their architecture can't go several levels deep. One solution is to resort to popup windows or lightbox displays to showcase deep-level photographic content.

A more novel solution is to make your site depth shallow, and simply feature your photography and video content as the background of your page, beneath your navigation and text content. The web site of the performance art band Fischerspooner does just that (**Figure 8.13**). There are no popup windows. The content is the actual background of the site. The plus and minus icons in the logo circle navigate through the different backgrounds. Most of the text information is included in a floating gray box that can be collapsed into an unobtrusive gray bar and dragged aside. All other content on top of the background image is collapsible. The logo circle itself is even movable.

Figure 8.13 fischerspooner.com

On certain pages, if there is more than one background image, a horizontal scrollbar allows you to scroll down and view all the images on that page. Some backgrounds are even comprised of multiple video clips that play simultaneously (**Figure 8.14**).

From an information architecture perspective, the site is hierarchically flat. It only has one level. The entire site is one big "gallery." fischerspooner.com reverses the standard function of a web site in order to showcase its imagery rather than its text. Foreground text becomes optional and inconsequential. Background imagery becomes the focal point.

Figure 8.14 fischerspooner.com

Surrealistic Landscapes

Fullscreen Fashion style isn't applicable only to photo portfolio sites. It can also be applied in conjunction with Flash to create surreal, immersive landscapes. The bottom of the browser serves as the ground plane of the scene; the top of the browser frames the sky.

A good example of this technique is the site for the musician Beck. Here, the landscape is not an outdoor one, but an interior, surreal, marionette stage (**Figure 8.15**). It features impossibly cobbled-together virtual jukeboxes that play various video and audio clips (**Figure 8.16**).

The Beck site was designed by the interactive design firm Hi-Res (who also designed the Dolce & Gabbana site mentioned earlier and The Fountain site, which I discuss in a moment). Hi-Res is adept at designing sensible, highly intuitive and innovative interfaces, but it excels at inventing surreal, delightfully confounding, imaginative ones. The Beck site falls into the latter category.

Figure 8.15 beck.com/default.aspx home page

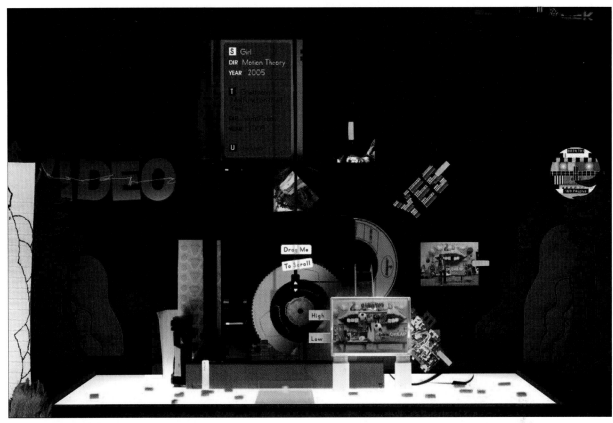

Figure 8.16 beck.com/default.aspx video section

Figure 8.17 sketch.uk.com (the parlour)

sketch.uk.com also features surreal interior landscapes. It showcases several themed dining rooms of the funky upscale London restaurant Sketch. Instead of displaying straightforward photographs of the rooms, each room is represented as an interactive toy tableau, a kind of diminutive Victorian diorama (**Figure 8.17**).

Clicking on different objects invokes different animations. Ultimately, when all the objects in a room are clicked, a collage of photographs from the real room and photographs of the tiny objects emerge (**Figure 8.18**). In each digital "room," the ground plane is implied but never clearly demarcated. These curious collages ephemerally reside in an imaginary, ungrounded, digital space.

The site provides its visitors with an alluring, pleasantly surreal foretaste of the restaurant without giving the entire dining experience away. Web visitors are compelled to visit the real restaurant, if only to sit down bodily in one of these quaint, fantastical rooms.

Figure 8.18 sketch.uk.com (the lecture room)

Finally, Canadian artist Myron Campbell provides a series of surreal exterior landscapes in his various experimental interactive projects. In "The Fragile Circus," we meet a menagerie of oddly animated creatures that exist on a landscape of collaged textile patterns (**Figure 8.19**). In "The Secret and The Wolf," we enter the world of a dandily dressed wolf and his private diary (**Figure 8.20**).

Both of these interactive experiments eschew text navigation. Instead, visitors can only proceed by clicking on objects in the animated Flash landscape. Campbell's scenes not only look surreal, they behave surrealistically.

Figure 8.19 notsosimpleton.com/TheFragileCircus/

Figure 8.20 glia.ca/vagus2008/artists/myronCampbell/wolf5.swf

Uses

The main use of Fullscreen Fashion style is obvious from the examples I've chosen: it is ideal for a photographer's portfolio site. It is also ideal for an architect's portfolio site, a fashion clothing site, and any other site where large, high resolution photography is the main content.

There are several online image portfolio services available that allow photographers to inexpensively (or freely) create online galleries of their work. Flickr is the social networking version of such services. The challenge for any commercial web designer is to create custom sites for clients that look and function better than these generic services.

The surreal landscape flavor of Fullscreen Fashion style is ideally suitable for a film promotion site. Not a site that simply has a trailer and a list of actor bios, but a site that creates a cross-media, backstory experience that complements the movie.

The interactive design jedi at Hi-Res have created a number of such sites for films like *Requiem for a Dream*, *Donnie Darko*, *Saw*, and the television series *Lost*. Their site for Darren Aronofsky's film *The Fountain* is a series of bristling, undulating, animated scenes from the movie (**Figure 8.21**), accompanied by cryptic audio. The edges of each landscape fade into darkness, giving the entire site a hallucinatory, visionary quality. The site acts like an interactive teaser for the film, giving away just enough to whet the visitor's appetite.

Figure 8.21 archive.hi-res.net/thefountain/experience/

Sites that contain streaming video content are also candidates for Fullscreen Fashion style. abc.com streams full versions of its episodes online in a special popup window. The window itself is 1000-pixels wide by 700-pixels high, but the embedded videos are only 700-pixels wide by 400-pixels high. Most people will expand the videos to fullscreen size once they load, but until then, how do you kill the remaining space? In the case of the *Lost* episode player, the background is filled with a fullscreen beachfront scene from the series.

Ultimately, Fullscreen Fashion style is appropriate for any site that wants to be bold and arresting. Creative Time is a good example. It funds public visual art projects often involving large-screen projections and billboards. Fullscreen Fashion style aptly transforms the site into a large, bold, unapologetic billboard amidst a web full of conservative, diminutive, text-centric sites.

● ● ●

When images are more important than text, new layouts and navigation schemes are required. There is still only one World Wide Web (the last time I checked), but there are thousands of different ways to use it. As bandwidth continues to increase, even more ways will continue to emerge.

However, simply because we *can* feature fullscreen video content, this doesn't mean that all sites will suddenly abandon text. The web doesn't want to become television, but neither does it have to remain *The New York Times*. Observe how news sites like cnn.com (and even faux news sites like theonion.com) have gradually increased their streaming video content. When the U.S. presidential debates are streamed live via MySpace(?!?), you know we're not in text-centric Kansas anymore.

Fullscreen Fashion style need not replace Late(st) Modern style in your web design toolbox, but it can supplement it. Fullscreen Fashion may be just the right tool for clients whose visuals are more important than their text.

THE SENSE OF PLEASURE
IN DRAWING A GOOD LINE,
WOULD REALLY, I THINK, BE
EDUCATION IN THE DUE SENSE
OF THE WORD FOR ALL SUCH
PEOPLE AS HAD THE GERMS OF
INVENTION IN THEM.[1]

—WILLIAM MORRIS

KEEP THE IRREGULARITIES
INCONSISTENT.[2]

—EDWARD FELLA

09 | *HAND-DRAWN ANALOG STYLE*

Web sites are usually associated with computers. People use computers to access them, and web designers use computers to make them. Not surprisingly, a lot of web sites look like they were conceived on computers. Their layouts are very regular, their right angles are mathematically perfect, their typography is digitally set, and their imagery is created using digital imaging tools like Photoshop and Illustrator.

But web sites don't have to be designed on computers any more than automobiles have to be designed with wrenches. You could design a website, create all its imagery, and even write all its code using a pencil and a sketchbook. Eventually you would have to scan the imagery and enter the code into a computer, but not until the very end of your design process.

Designers who practice Hand-Drawn Analog style don't write code in their sketchbooks, but they do create a lot of their web imagery by hand away from the computer. *Analog* in this sense simply means nondigital. The source visuals for Hand-Drawn Analog sites are not created with digital tools. *Hand-drawn* means these visuals aren't painted, offset printed, or photo-collaged, but actually drawn by a human hand.

The source imagery for sites designed using this style can eventually be digitally colored, but the creation of the imagery begins with a pen or pencil. Once you scan or digitally photograph your drawings, you should avoid vectorizing and post-processing your lines too much in Illustrator, lest you wind up with another style that I call *1970s Dayglow Vector style* (think glittery, iron-on t-shirts featuring Trans Ams, disco vans, and California surfers, with lots of cartoonish shooting stars in the background). There's nothing wrong with 1970's Dayglow Vector style; it just has a smoother, more regularized, more digitally processed line than Hand-Drawn Analog style. The line of the latter style is more irregular and idiosyncratic—more human.

HAND-DRAWN ANALOG STYLE ALWAYS

CONVEYS THE PERSONALIZED TOUCH

OF A SPECIFIC HUMAN HAND.

Influences

Hand-Drawn Analog style is influenced by artists like Aubrey Beardsley, Edward Gorey, and Ralph Steadman, who draw with a recognizable and intentionally expressive line. Their art is not just in their subject matter, but also in the personality of their own hand-drawn line. Hand-Drawn Analog style is also influenced by homemade, hand-drawn, American signage and the hand-drawn typography of Edward Fella.

Most Hand-Drawn Analog designers began doodling in the margins of their English notebooks at an early age. They don't necessarily trace their personal influence directly back to the artists I mention. Nevertheless, these artists are the historical godfathers of this hand-drawn approach to web design.

Expressive Line Illustrations

As early as the late 1800s, Aubrey Beardsley was pioneering a recognizable illustration style that would influence a host of 20th Century artists. His drawn line was organic and free flowing; his human figures were often elongated; and his compositions were frequently black and white with few intermediary gray tones. Beardsley's gothic subject matter influenced later illustrators like Edward Gorey, whose compulsive, childlike lines and simple crosshatch shadings contrasted disturbingly with his macabre subject matter. Ralph Steadman rounds out this trilogy of influences with a loose, sprawling pen-and-ink line that perfectly coveys his stream-of-consciousness approach to his subject matter.

These three master illustrators are immediately recognizable by the personality of their line. Given only a fragment of a Gorey illustration, a tree and some grass or a bird on a hedge, his particular style is unmistakably evident. The same is true of Beardsley and Steadman.

Hand-Drawn Analog designers don't necessarily imitate the specific styles of these illustrators, but they do place a priority on the expressive personality of the hand-drawn line. They choose to leave visible waverings, ink splotches, smudges, and other telltale irregularities of the physical drawing event. They don't use the computer to regularize their line. Hand-Drawn Analog style always conveys the personalized touch of a specific human hand.

Hand-Drawn Vernacular Lettering

Edward Fella is arguably *the* contemporary master of hand-drawn typography. Like Wolfgang Weingart, Fella learned the craft of typesetting well before he began experimentally pushing its boundaries. Fella began warping and twisting phototypography, and then moved on to hand-draw his own freeform letters (**Figure 9.1**).

Fella's book *Letters on America* features his own snapshots of "vernacular" American lettering—hand-painted signage by amateur, untrained, un-designers. Rather than critique this work, Fella celebrates it.

Fella's own experimental hand-lettering is more like art than commercial design. His compositions are 2D sculptures cobbled together from modified, customized letterforms to

Figure 9.1 Edward Fella. Page 103 from "Lettering Book Ball Pt. & Pencil 2003."

visually express the meaning of the words they spell. Fella's work reminds me of Howard Finster's junkyard sculptures. It is wonderful, idiosyncratic, American folk art typography.

Hand-Drawn Analog web designers also draw their own expressive letters. Hand-lettering is mostly applied to menu links and background images. Large paragraphs of text are still set in HTML typography for legibility and browser-indexing purposes. Any hand-drawn word can be scanned and saved as a .gif, and any .gif can be turned into a link, so menu letterforms need not be limited by digital typography.

Sketching and Doodling

Hand-Drawn Analog style is not only influenced by the four great artists above, it is also influenced by hours of sketching and doodling in the margins of high school notebooks. This kind of drawing has less to do with illustrating a central subject and more to do with decorative patterning. The goal is simply to enjoyably pass time by filling in all available marginal space. Geometric patterns, unfolding flower petals, shooting stars, rainbows, unicorns, and ligers—nothing is off limits as long as the pleasure of drawing is being experienced by the doodler.

Hand-Drawn Analog web designers apply a restrained version of this doodling approach to their backgrounds and margins. Extreme Hand-Drawn Analog sites feel like a celebration of decoration for its own sake. These sites are the antithesis of sterile and generic web design.

Characteristics

The main and obvious characteristic of Hand-Drawn Analog sites is that they are hand-drawn. It may be that only the letters, the decorative background embellishments, or the central illustrations are hand-drawn, or it may be a combination of all three, but at least some aspect of the site is drawn by hand. Sometimes only a wayfinding "you are here" navigational marker is hand-drawn. Sometimes the entire site draws itself via Flash animation.

Hand-Drawn Analog sites also feature analog paper textures, ink blots, peeling stickers—anything to give them a less digital, more physical appearance. Although these sites feature textural irregularities and a freeform line, they are usually laid out according to a grid pattern. The hand-drawn line acts as a counterpoint to the grid, making it seem less rigid.

Most of the sites featured as examples in this chapter contain more than one characteristic of the Hand-Drawn Analog style. I have organized them according to the characteristic they most exemplify.

Illustrations and Embellishments

The site for the undergraduate program at Biola University is a classic example of Hand-Drawn Analog web design. It features a hand-lettered menu, a textured paper background, a central hand-drawn illustration, and hand-drawn decorative embellishments throughout the site (**Figure 9.2**).

The line of the hand-drawn embellishments matches the line of the central illustration.

Figure 9.2 biola.edu/undergrad/

Indeed, these embellishments seem to seep out from the central illustration into other areas of the page. Note how the hand-drawn words break out of the square content areas in the right column, making these areas seem less rigid.

Hand-Drawn Analog style makes the site more playful and less formal without adversely affecting the clear presentation of its content. Paragraphs of text are still perfectly legible; photographs are clearly discernible; and the main menu is easily navigable. The Biola undergraduate site achieves visual personality without sacrificing functionality.

Letters

Not every single letter on a Hand-Drawn Analog site needs to be hand-drawn. Full paragraphs of body text can and should be set in HTML-CSS typography so that the text is selectable, legible, and search-engine indexable. Yes, Comic Sans is a browser safe font that may seem like handwriting in some sort of twisted and sadistic alternate universe. You may be tempted to use it for your paragraph text. Don't, or you will wind up with something that looks like a bad version of 1996 Dirt style rather than anything having to do with Hand-Drawn Analog style.

Hand-drawn lettering is best applied to menu text and header text. Menu text often appears at the top of the page, so it immediately establishes the hand-drawn look of the site. Header text appears throughout the page, injecting hand-drawn characters amidst larger paragraphs of HTML typography. Hand-Drawn lettering can also can be applied to the background of the site as an illustrative element, as if someone were scribbling personal notes. Make sure you apply it sparingly and subtly, lest your background words appear too prominently and are mistaken for linkable menu text.

Excluding Comic Sans, feel free to use a nice handwriting font for your hand-drawn lettering. Handwriting fonts are often named after their designers. For instance, "Cina Hand" is the name of a font created by designer Mike Cina based on his own handwriting.

You won't be able to use handwriting fonts as HTML typography (since they aren't "browser-safe"), but you can set your words in Photoshop or Illustrator and then save them as .gifs. Handwriting fonts look less irregular than hand-drawn words on paper. All the *a*'s in a handwriting font will look the same, whereas your hand-drawn *a*'s will all look slightly different. Choose one or the other (or both) based on the effect you want to achieve.

Psyop (a multimedia design firm specializing in animation) uses hand-lettering on its portfolio site. Its main menu items are hand-drawn, letter by letter, while its submenu items are set in a handwriting font (**Figure 9.3**). The words *new, platinum select, propaganda, archive, operations, contact, client login* and *check out my sisters* are all individually hand-drawn. Every other word on the page is set in a handwriting font. The hand-drawn words in the main menu make the handwriting font in the submenu seem less digital and more irregular.

Figure 9.3 psyop.tv

Other subtle elements add to the overall hand-drawn feel of the Psyop page. There is a slight crease in the background of the site about halfway down the page. The background image is actually an image of physical paper. This crease adds a hint of analog texture without overwhelming the featured content. Even the borders and buttons of the video player window are hand-drawn. Hand-Drawn Analog is an apt style for a site showcasing these illustrated animations.

Background Killer: Paper Textures, Marginal Doodles

The background of most Hand-Drawn Analog sites begins with a scan or a digital photograph of actual paper. This digital image can be further textured in Photoshop by adding other semi-transparent layers of texture on top of it. The source paper should be worn, wrinkled, and distressed enough to look like paper rather than simply an off-white background color.

Paper textures alone may not be enough to creatively kill extra background space, so illustrative doodles on the paper are often added. These doodles can be ornate, decorative patterns derived from flowers and plants, like Arts & Crafts wallpaper. They can be childlike, playful sketches of shooting stars and rainbows. Or they can be whatever you decide to draw. Just make sure the patterns you choose sensibly embellish the content of your site.

Wayfinding Markers

Hand-Drawn Analog style need not overwhelm a site. Aspects of it can actually be applied very subtly to great effect. threadless.com is a good example. Its logo is hand-written, and it uses a hand-drawn circle and arrow in its menu navigation system (**Figure 9.4**).

Mousing over any main menu section reveals its submenu sections (**Figure 9.5**). The circle acts as a wayfinding marker to show visitors where they are and where they might be going. The arrow acts as a hierarchical bridge between the main menu and the various submenus. In addition to adding a hand-drawn look to the site, these menu wayfinding markers actually increase the navigability of the site.

The site is laid out on a clean modernist grid, appropriate for a catalog site with a lot of content. The backend functionality of the site is highly sophisticated. Yet the site still feels inviting, illustrated, and slightly homemade. This look and feel is appropriate for Threadless, a t-shirt company that is really more like an online community of graphic designers. The t-shirts are designed by anyone, voted on by everyone via the website, and the most popular shirts are printed and sold.

threadless.com needs to look reputable and professional to instill consumer confidence, but it also has to look D.I.Y. and inviting before it will encourage community participation. This subtle application of Hand-Drawn Analog style to an otherwise clean and modern layout is the perfect solution for this particular site.

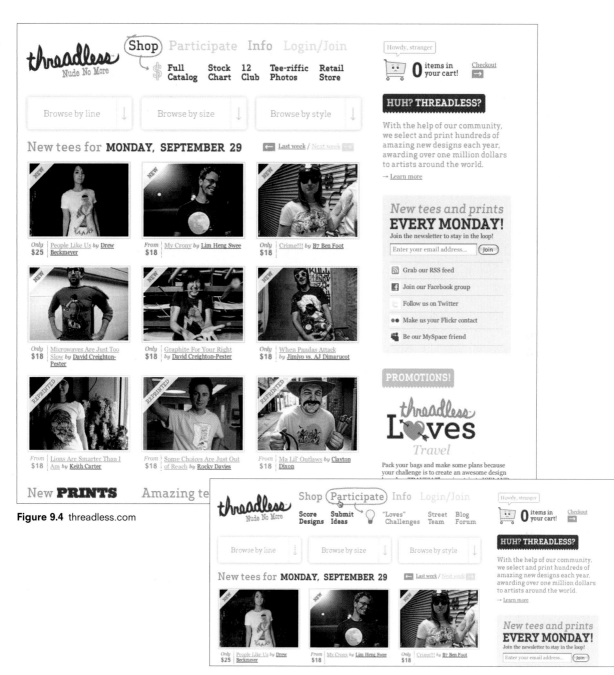

Figure 9.4 threadless.com

Figure 9.5 threadless.com

Figure 9.6 satsu.co.uk

Analog Textures

Hand-Drawn Analog style is not primarily about physical textures, but physical textures do play a part in eroding the digital feel of a site. There are all sorts of textures that could be scanned and used as the background of a web site—oil paint on canvas, watercolor paint on paper, marbled paper, wood, rust, or chrome—but the ones most appropriate for Hand-Drawn Analog style are sketchbook paper, tracing paper, stationary paper (particularly handmade), Japanese rice paper, even architectural blueprint paper. Anything someone might draw on with a pencil or pen.

Lined notebook paper and graph paper are less appropriate, since they were overused as "page" backgrounds in the early days of the web and now connote 1996 Dirt style. Creases, stains, ink blots, rips, and deckled edges add further evidence of physicality. Creating these textured effects by layering multiple images in Photoshop is perfectly acceptable. You shouldn't have to spend years perfectly aging and distressing your ideal piece of physical paper.

The colors of your paper textures can vary, but they will probably be browns, tans, off-whites, and ochres. A perfectly white background (with a hexadecimal value of #FFFFFF) is a telltale sign that something was digitally made. Few things in the nonscreen world are perfectly white. Even a sheet of white paper when scanned will not be perfectly, uniformly, and mathematically white.

If you want to add hand-drawn decorative embellishments to your background, simply draw them on the piece of paper you wish to use as your background texture, and then scan or digitally photograph the whole piece of paper. You might want to draw some decorations and then lightly erase them, leaving a faint trace. This adds an additional layer of physical texture. Prepare your background texture in Photoshop to tile seamlessly (or not so seamlessly), save it as a .jpg file, and set it as the background image of your page.

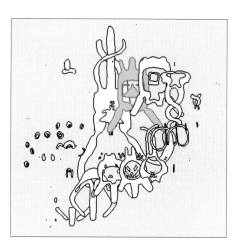

The portfolio site for the British design firm Satsu achieves an admirable level of background and foreground analog texture (**Figure 9.6**). Its logo and its menu strip look like physical stickers that are peeling off the page. Inkblots, decorative embellishments, and hand-written notes add texture to the already textured and distressed background paper image. Satsu's slogan, hand-written in red marker beside its logo, reads like a motto for the Hand-Drawn Analog style: "Digital Design, Hand-Crafted."

Animated Drawing

Some designers use Flash to animate their hand-drawn illustrations, imbuing them with even more character and expressive personality. Artist James Patterson of presstube.com is the acknowledged master of this form of expressive hand-drawn animation. His animations are immediately recognizable by their nervously playful line and their rapid, stream-of-consciousness motion (**Figure 9.7**). Although Patterson's original sketches are translated to vector lines in order to be animated in Flash, they retain the rough, irregular feel of their original hand-drawn state.

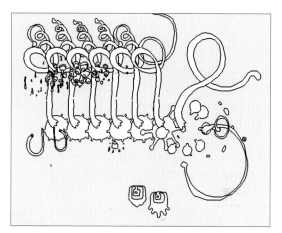

Figure 9.7 presstube.com/projects.php?id=218 in two different states

Figure 9.8 krening.com/lurk/ in two different states

Patterson's strange doodles appear, transform, evaporate, and reappear as if they were streaming directly from the artist's brain in real-time. The drawing process itself is animated, as if these illustrations were being drawn before our eyes ... by an eight-handed creature drawing at the speed of thought. The screenshots in this book hardly do the work justice. Visit presstube.com for the full experience.

Designer, illustrator, and artist Karen Ingram experiments with a different kind of hand-drawn animation at krening.com. She uses Flash to animate several pastel drawings of the same face making different expressions (**Figure 9.8**).

The eyes blink and glance sideways; the nose twitches, the lips purse and grimace. Each drawing subtly fades into the next as the animation progresses. It looks less like a slideshow of static drawings and more like a living face. As an extra touch, small, animated gnats perpetually buzz around the background flowers.

The face is obviously drawn rather than photographed. As it moves, the hand-drawn pastel lines seem to blur and smudge, as if the drawing had willed itself to life, its motions altering the very material with which it was drawn. The face perpetually shifts and twitches, patiently enduring the gnats as it waits for the user to click something. This animated drawing of a human face adds life, charm, and personality to the page in a way that a mere video clip of a human face could not.

Uses

Hand-Drawn Analog style is suitable for a rock band site or a pop singer site. Bands and singers have expressive human personalities. The timbre of a famous singer's voice is immediately distinguishable. The sound of a famous band is immediately recognizable. Hand-Drawn illustration can give a web site that same kind of recognizable, personal, human quality. Hand-Drawn Analog style seems more appropriate for showcasing acoustic and folk music, and less appropriate for showcasing electronic and computer-based music. But of course there are exceptions depending on the band.

Hand-Drawn Analog style also has been successfully used for a number of comedy movie promotional sites: *Napoleon Dynamite* (www2.foxsearchlight.com/napoleondynamite/epk), *Juno* (foxsearchlight.com/juno), and *Year of the Dog* (yearofthedogmovie.com). Each site presents the world of the movie from the perspective of its main character. If Napoleon Dynamite designed a website based on his own sketchbook, what would it look like? This approach works for comedies (teen comedies in particular), but you wouldn't want to design the *Die Hard* 5 web site in Hand-Drawn Analog style.

Finally, any site marketing handcrafted services or goods is an obvious candidate for Hand-Drawn Analog style. The site literally could be selling handicrafts. Or it could be selling custom-designed t-shirts. In the case of the Biola University undergraduate site, a private school is selling a handcrafted, personalized education as opposed to an impersonal, institutional education. Whatever the handmade product or service, you want the site to seem well crafted without seeming juvenile.

● ● ●

In an era of prefabricated web design templates, services, and interchangeable modules, Hand-Drawn Analog style injects a personalized human element into the look and feel of web design. The expressive gestures of a hand-drawn line can be an integral part of web design. The style can be applied with varying degrees of intensity depending on the nature of the project. Some sites may only need hand-drawn wayfinding markers. Others may benefit from hand-drawn everything—lettering, decorative embellishments, analog textures, and animations.

Since most web sites still look like they were made with computers, Hand-Drawn Analog Sites are guaranteed to stand out. That is until Adobe develops a Hand-Drawn plug-in for Dreamweaver, but that may be a while.

STYLE IS A DECISION ABOUT HOW WE LIVE. STYLE IS NOT SUPERFICIAL. IT IS A PHILOSOPHICAL PROJECT OF THE DEEPEST ORDER.

—BRUCE MAU

10 | *STYLE MATTERS*

In 1996, the web was littered with black-and-yellow-striped animated .gifs reveling in metaphors of road construction (**Figure 10.1**). "This site under construction" was the default home page disclaimer, until everyone realized that the inherent nature of the web was that it would be perpetually under construction. And of course, the web is still under construction—we are still making it, and making it up.

The Web Still Awaits Invention

Computer scientist Alan Kay famously observed, "The best way to predict the future is to invent it."[1] The web still awaits invention, yet listening to many web design pundits, you would think the web is a 400-year-old medium with rules, guidelines, and principles all firmly entrenched. This is simply not the case. Commerce changes. Business models change. Media changes. The web itself is perpetually changing into something other than what it currently is.

As a medium, the web is particularly malleable and adaptable. Architecture is less malleable. A physical building has to stand up under the force of gravity. It has to provide physical space in which people can dwell. It (usually) has to keep the rain out.

But on the web, there is no gravity. There is no weather (unless your cable line gets knocked down in a storm). A building in the online virtual world Second Life, for example, can be ridiculously impractical and contrary to the laws of materials, physics, and gravity—yet it will still stand (**Figure 10.2**). Likewise, if you build an imaginative cloud-castle of a site, unjustifiable to the quantifiable rules of user-testing and eyeball-tracking data, it may stand nonetheless.

But what about information architecture? Information architecture is merely analogous to architecture. It's not "real" architecture. It has more to do with language and cognition than with bodies and space. Is web information architecture limited by material constraints? Definitely. Think about the protocols, languages, and standards that are being developed all the time. However, Extensible Hypertext Markup Language (XHTML) is a lot more malleable than steel. And web design best practices are a lot more malleable than skyscraper construction best practices.

With an awareness that we are still inventing the web, I want to conclude with a few general principles to keep in mind as you apply the styles defined in this book to your own projects, and as you develop new styles of your own.

Web Designers Matter

Because the web is still a (relatively) new and inherently malleable medium, web designers have the potential to dramatically alter it. And now that more than half the world's population is using the web, suddenly web designers are in a position to have an even greater impact.

Figure 10.1 "Under construction" animated .gif

However, we won't change or advance anything if we don't believe the web *can* be changed.

If professional web designers believe that people are preconditioned to favor the least common denominator in design, then that is what we will end up delivering. If we believe that design is mere embellishment, having nothing to do with the way people live, then we will fail to advocate for invigorating, challenging design.

Figure 10.2 Scripted Second Life architecture by Erik Andrén

But if we believe that design matters, and that people's lives can be changed by design, then we hold the possibility of changing the world (or at least doing better work). Fortunately, people are more malleable, flexible, and reconfigurable than we might initially think.

Usability Experts Don't Always Matter

Usability experts presuppose that people are fundamentally static and limited in their ability to change. They assume that the best way to design is to reduce human behavior to basic principles, to study these principles, and then to construct design rules that accommodate these principles.

Quantifying scientists are usability experts' best friends. They do research on things like eye-tracking, calculate the results, and publish them in books. But simply measuring *where* a person's eyes look on a web page doesn't really tell us much about *how* people process and experience the information on that page.

Computer interface designer Joy Mountford once lamented, "When the computer stares back at you, it sees you as one eye and one finger"[2]. And yet we humans are not simply disembodied eyes and brains floating in our Aeron chairs, nor are we Pavlovian subjects conditioned to react to a limited set of universal design principles. Visceral, emotional, experimental interactive design will always have a place on the web, because humans are complex beings who respond to holistic sensory experiences.

Style Makes Life

As I've already mentioned, style is nothing more than a way of doing something. For a designer, style is a way of creating that produces a particular set of forms. Fresh styles produce fresh forms. And if function follows form as readily as form follows function, then fresh functions follow fresh forms. (Say that fast five times!)

There is a wrongheaded idea that style is simply a minor surface embellishment that has nothing to do with function. In reality, style doesn't merely embellish life; style makes life. Designer Bruce Mau elaborates:

> "Life doesn't simply happen to us; we produce it. That's what style is. It's producing life. Rather than accepting that life is something that we passively receive, accept, or endure, I believe that life is something we generate... . Style is a decision about how we live. Style is not superficial. It is a philosophical project of the deepest order."[3]

Experimental design holds the potential to modify human function. With our world and our media changing so rapidly, we can no longer afford to be too closely wed to any single, dogmatic design approach. In this climate of change, experimental design becomes a lot more practical than its conservative detractors originally thought. If the best way to predict the future is to invent it, then design styles invent the forms that make the future.

The Craft of Web Design

Ultimately, after all the theoretical and philosophical justifications for experimental design, your next project will succeed or fail not based on the theory you used, but in its practicality.

This book is written primarily for working web designers, because design is a pragmatic craft. Demographic research and conceptual predesigning are of course invaluable; but in and of themselves, they aren't actually design. Design happens in the space of the page (even the digital page). Simply thinking conceptually is not enough. The way to really "know" something in design is through creating it.

Designer Dan Saffer notes that anyone can have a concept, but not everyone can execute a design:

> "It is in the detail work that design really happens—that the clever, delightful moments of a design occur. Those are as important, if not more so, than the concept itself. The details are where we earn our money and our respect, and the details can only be worked out through making stuff."[4]

After all my idealizing about designers changing the world, you now have return to work and actually make something. Excellent! The fact that you are putting actual design on the web is crucial. As Apple CEO Steve Jobs preaches, "Real artists ship."[5] The best way to improve the commercial web is to design a better commercial web, site by site.

As you return to the work of making web sites, I hope the examples in this book will remain "in the room" with you, looking over your shoulder, raising the bar of your expectations, challenging you to risk more often, and inspiring you to continually care about your craft.

As web designers, it's our web. We are the ones who get to make it up. Let's not make it bland. In the face of encroaching deadlines, low budgets, difficult clients, and unsympathetic bosses, I encourage you to let the forces of each project shape the stylistic forms that best suit that project—whether those forces are safe, risky, or something entirely different.

Finally, in the words of graphic design pioneer and Catholic nun Corita Kent, "Be happy whenever you can manage it. Enjoy yourself. It's lighter than you think."[6]

Design is truly sexy. Even designing the content management system for a plumbing web site is (kind of) sexy. It beats actual plumbing! Design can be a noble and ennobling profession, and web design is a legitimate form of design. If you've lost your passion for design, do all you can to regain it. Your design work will improve as a result, so will the web, and so will the world. What you make matters.

Endnotes

CHAPTER 2

1. Emily Dickinson, The Poems of Emily Dickinson: Reading Edition. ed. R. W. Franklin (Cambridge, Mass.: The Belknap Press of Harvard University Press, 1999), 116 [Franklin #260].

2. Lawrence Weiner in Seth Siegelaub's, January 5-31, 1969 (New York: Seth Siegelaub, 1969), n.p.; quoted in Liz Kotz, Words To Be Looked At: Language in 1960s Art (Cambridge, Mass.: The MIT Press, 2007), 199.

3. Johanna Drucker, "Un-Visual and Conceptual," Open Letter: A Canadian Journal of Writing and Theory, Twelfth Series, No. 7 (2005), ed. Barbara Cole and Lori Emerso. Available from www.ubu.com/papers/kg_ol_drucker.html

CHAPTER 3

1. Wolfgang Weingart, *My Way To Typography* (Baden, Switzerland: Lars Müller, 2000), 101.

2. Three good books on the grid are:

- Josef Müller-Brockmann's *Grid Systems in Graphic Design: A Visual Communication Manual for Graphic Designers, Typographers, and Three Dimensional Designers* (Niederteufen, Switzerland: Verlag Arthur Niggli, 1981). The classic text on grid systems. Both practical and poetically optimistic.

- Willi Kunz's *Typography: Macro- and Microaesthetics* (Sulgen, Switzerland: Niggli, 2000). Approaches grid systems from a more layered, deconstructive perspective. Written by a master who uses his own meticulous work as figure examples.

- Timothy Samara's *Making and Breaking the Grid: A Graphic Design Layout Workshop* (Gloucester, MA: Rockport Publishers, 2005). Harmonizes and integrates Müller-Brockmann and Kunz. Contains a concise history of the modernist grid and a plethora of commercial examples of grid construction and deconstruction, complete with diagrams and commentary.

3. For more on the pixel-height approach to "baseline grid" web typesetting, see Wilson Miller's "Setting Type on the Web to a Baseline Grid," A List Apart, April 2007. Available from www.alistapart.com/articles/settingtypeontheweb/

4. For more on the em-height approach to "baseline grid" web typesetting, see Richard Rutter's "Compose to a Vertical Rhythm," 24 Ways, 2006. Available from http://24ways.org/2006/compose-to-a-vertical-rhythm/ Also Mark Boulton's "Five Simple Steps to Designing Grid Systems: Part 5." Available from www.markboulton.co.uk/journal/comments/five_simple_steps_to_designing_grid_systems_part_5/

5. A standard framework for CSS grids is the Grid Component of the Yahoo User Interface Library, available from http://developer.yahoo.com/yui/grids/ (cf: Dav Glass' YUI Grid Builder at http://developer.yahoo.com/yui/grids/builder/). Olav Bjørkøy's Blueprint framework is particularly popular and robust. It is available from http://code.google.com/p/blueprintcss/ A good introduction to CSS frameworks is Jeff Croft's "Frameworks for Designers," *A List Apart* 2007. Available from www.alistapart.com/articles/frameworksfordesigners/ Finally, an instructive case study in the practical application of grid systems to web design is Khoi Vinh and Mark Boulton's "Grids are Good" presentation at SXSW *Interactive*, March 2007. The slides are available from www.subtraction.com/pics/0703/grids_are_good.pdf

6. Weingart's teacher Emil Ruder and Weingart's student Willi Kunz preferred to worked with just one typeface, the versatile Univers. Grid-master Massimo Vignelli prefers to work with just five faces (Bodoni, Century Expanded, Garamond no. 3, Times Roman, and Helvetica).

7. The browser-safe fonts that currently work on all operating system platforms in all browsers are Arial, Arial Black, Comic Sans MS, Courier New, Georgia, Impact, Times New Roman, Trebuchet MS, and Verdana—a hilariously rag-tag group of typefaces, mostly owing to the logic of the Microsoft operating system. Comic Sans is of course evil and should be avoided by anyone other than company secretaries designing holiday office party flyers. Times New Roman is the classic serif face for web body text. Verdana is arguably the most legible sans-serif face for web body text. With so many people using Verdana for body text, Arial can be a nice sans-serif substitute (not as nice as Helvetica, but thanks to Bill Gates, Helvetica ain't on the browser-safe list). Times New Roman, set large and bold with negative letterspacing, can be an elegant and novel approach for header type. Suggested CSS is:

```
h1 {
font-family: "Times New Roman", serif;
font-size: 52px;
line-height: 46px;
letter-spacing: -2px;
font-weight: bold;
}
```

Trebuchet (drawn by Vincent Connare, the same typographer who created Comic Sans) is a beautiful, underutilized sans-serif face. It's too peculiar to use for large paragraphs of body text, but it makes unique header and sub-header text. A useful resource for browser-safe HTML typography is www.typetester.maratz.com

CHAPTER 6

1. For a more philosophical analysis of translucency and glitter, read Olia Lialina's "Vernacular Web 2," August 2007. Available from contemporary-home-computing.org/vernacular-web-2/

2. Olia Lialina, "A Vernacular Web: The Indigenous and the Barbarians," notes from a talk delivered at the Decade of Web Design Conference, Amsterdam, January 2005. Available from art.teleportacia.org/observation/vernacular/

CHAPTER 7

1. Jorge Luis Borges, "Of Exactitude in Science," in *A Universal History of Infamy* (London: Penguin Books, 1975).

CHAPTER 9

1. William Morris, "The Lesser Arts," in *Stories in Prose, Stories in Verse, Shorter Poems, Lectures and Essays,* ed. G. D. H. Cole (London: The Nonesuch Press, 1948), 510.

2. Edward Fella from a poster he designed in 1993. The full text reads, "Keep the irregularities inconsistent, variously differentiated, and otherwise unmatched in all manner of ways and variety of sorts."

CHAPTER 10

1. Supposedly uttered at a Xerox Palo Alto Research Center meeting in 1971.

2. Camille Utterback, "Unusual Positions – Embodied Interaction with Symbolic Spaces," in *First Person: New Media as Story, Performance, and Game*, ed. Noah Wardrip-Fruin and Pat Harrigan (Cambridge, Mass: The MIT Press, 2004), 218.

3. Bruce Mau, *Life Style* (New York: Phaidon, 2000), 27. Cf: www.moma.org/exhibitions/2008/elasticmind/

4. Dan Saffer, "Making Stuff vs. Making Stuff Up," *A Brief Message*, November 2007. Available from http://abriefmessage.com/2007/11/01/saffer/

5. Steven Levy, *Insanely Great: The Life and Times of Macintosh, the Computer That Changed Everything* (New York: Penguin, 2000), 165.

6. Corita Kent, "Immaculate Heart College Art Department Rules." Available from http://lab404.com/misc/wwcd.jpg Cf: www.corita.org

Figure Credits

CHAPTER 4
1. Walker Art Center
   Designer: Brent Gustafson
2. Linn Olofsdotter
   olofsdotter.com
3. New Museum
4. New Museum
5. Design/concept: Catalogtree
   CMS: Systemantics
6. Design/concept: Catalogtree
   CMS: Systemantics
7. Constant vzw
   Designer: Femke Snelting
8. Galeria Eva Presenhuber, Zurich
9. Artwork: Scipio Schneider
   scipioschneider.com
10. Galeria Eva Presenhuber, Zurich
11. Erik Johan Worsoe Eriksen / Marius Watz
12. Erik Johan Worsoe Eriksen / Marius Watz
13. Erik Johan Worsoe Eriksen / Marius Watz
14. Design: Flat Inc.
    flat.com
15. Design: Flat Inc.
    flat.com
16. Designer: Lifelong Friendship Society,
    Brooklyn, NY
17. Designer: Lifelong Friendship Society,
    Brooklyn, NY

CHAPTER 5
1. Abstraction Now
   Designer: Nik Thönen (re-p.org)
2. Dead Skin Press
   Designer: Ksenya Samarskaya
   (samarskaya.com)
3. Maiko Gubler
   mongrelnation.com

4. Marc Kremers
5. Abstraction Now
   Designer: Nik Thönen (re-p.org)
6. F A B R I C A
7. F A B R I C A
8. FILE festival internacional de linguagem
   electrônica
   www.file.org.br
   Founders and organizers: Paula Perissinotto
   & Ricardo Barreto, Brasil
9. Universal Everything
10. Universal Everything
11. Universal Everything
12. Spectator Books Team
    artasinstantidea.com

CHAPTER 6
1. Bruce Lawson
3. Blogger
   Designer: Doug Bowman
4. Pimp My Profile
   Designer: bnbthatsme
5. Concept: Big Active Ltd (bigactive.com)
   Art direction: Gerard Saint, Mat Maitland,
   Beck
   Design: Mat Maitland
   Sticker images: Jody Barton, Juliette Cezzar,
   Estelle & Simon, David Foldvari Genevieve
   Gauckler, Michael Gillette, Jasper Goodall,
   Mercedes Helnwein, Han Lee, Mat Maitland,
   Ari Michelson, Parra, Melanie Pullen, Gay
   Ribisi, Aleksey Shirokov, Will Sweeney, Kam
   Tang, Adam Tullie, Kensei Yabuno, Vania
   Zouravliov
   Artist coordination: Greg Burne, Richard
   Newton
6. Curt Cloninger

CHAPTER 7

1. Constant vzw
   Designer: Femke Snelting
2. Marc Kremers
3. WEFAIL, Martin Hughes/Jordan Stone
4. WEFAIL, Martin Hughes/Jordan Stone
5. PLURAL DESIGN
6. PLURAL DESIGN
7. Chris Molinski/The Art Gallery of Knoxville
8. Leo Burnett Company, Inc.
9. Leo Burnett Company, Inc.
10. Leo Burnett Company, Inc.
11. Leo Burnett Company, Inc.
12. WEFAIL, Martin Hughes/Jordan Stone
13. WEFAIL, Martin Hughes/Jordan Stone
14. WEFAIL, Martin Hughes/Jordan Stone
15. XIIN
16. XIIN
17. XIIN
18. tokyoplastic.com
19. The Good, The Bad & The Queen

CHAPTER 8

1. Creative Time
   Background image from *The Waterboard Thrill Ride* by Steve Powers, 2008.
   Photo: David B. Smith
2. Creative Time
3. Uwe Ditz
4. Uwe Ditz
5. Miles Aldridge
6. Miles Aldridge
7. Design: Hi-Res! (hi-res.net)
8. Design: Hi-Res! (hi-res.net)
9. TOCA ME

10. TOCA ME
11. Isabel Pettinato
12. Isabel Pettinato
13. FISCHERSPOONER
14. FISCHERSPOONER
15. Design: Hi-Res! (hi-res.net)
16. Design: Hi-Res! (hi-res.net)
17. sketch
    Designer: Katya Bonnenfant
18. sketch
    Designer: Katya Bonnenfant
19. myron campbell (notsosimpleton)
20. myron campbell (notsosimpleton)
21. Design: Hi-Res! (hi-res.net)

CHAPTER 9

1. Edward Fella
2. Biola University
3. PSYOP
4. skinnyCorp
5. skinnyCorp
6. Satsu Limited
7. James Patterson
8. © Karen S. Ingram

CHAPTER 10

2. Erik Andrén/LOL Architects

Sites Featured in This Book

NO STYLE

modernista.com
indexhibit.com
hit-studio.co.uk
sarahgerats.be
markreynolds.ca
francescaperani.com
we-make-money-not-art.com
lab404.com/work

LATE(ST) MODERN STYLE

designforfreedom.com
flat.com
helmutlang.com
christinewoditschka.com
katharinagrosse.com
kindcompany.com
poccuo.com
pepkarsten.com
roomstudio.net
deform-group.com
serviceisgood.com
nasher.duke.edu

PSYCHEDELIC MINIMALIST STYLE

newmedia.walkerart.org/nmiwiki
olofsdotter.com
newmuseum.org
catalogtree.net
constantvzw.org/vj10/
www.presenhuber.com
generatorx.no
pbs.org/art21
lifelongfriendshipsociety.com

DOT MATRIX STYLE

abstraction-now.at
deadskinpress.com
bonsaimai.de
tex-server.org/3/
abstraction-now.at/MATHS_IN_MOTION/
fabricafeatures.com
file.org.br
everyoneforever.com
advancedbeauty.org
spectormag.net

1996 DIRT STYLE

csszengarden.com/?cssfile=http://
    www.brucelawson.co.uk/zen/sample.css
pimp-my-profile.com
amazon.com/gp/customer-media/
    product-gallery/B000HIVO64/
blingee.com

CORKBOARD SPRAWL STYLE

constantvzw.org
tex-server.org
billyharveymusic.com
pluralplural.com
theartgalleryofknoxville.com
leoburnett.ca
wefail.com/xgames/
xiiin.com/idol_ani.asp
tokyoplastic.com
thegoodthebadandthequeen.com

FULLSCREEN FASHION STYLE
creativetime.org
uwe-ditz.com
milesaldridge.com
www.dolcegabbana.com/dg/
toca-me.com
smo-smo.com
fischerspooner.com
beck.com/default.aspx
sketch.uk.com
notsosimpleton.com/TheFragileCircus/
glia.ca/vagus2008/artists/myronCampbell/
  wolf5.swf
archive.hi-res.net/thefountain/experience/

HAND-DRAWN ANALOG STYLE
biola.edu/undergrad/
psyop.tv
threadless.com
satsu.co.uk
presstube.com
krening.com/lurk/
www2.foxsearchlight.com/napoleondynamite/
  epk/
foxsearchlight.com/juno/
yearofthedogmovie.com

INDEX

scale, web page, 123–124

screen colors, print vs., 73

scrolling. *see also* horizontal scrolling; vertical scrolling

    printed scrolls influencing, 124

    unbounded Corkboard Sprawl layout, 126–131

"The Secret and the Wolf" (Campbell), 159, 161

serif font, 62

serviceisgood.com, 66–67

shallow site depth, Fullscreen Fashion style, 154–155

signage

    American, 168

    modernist New York subway, 45

site depth, Fullscreen Fashion sites, 154–155

Site Flash, 133

sketch.uk, 158–159

sketching, Hand-Drawn Analog style, 170

smo-smo.com, 152–153

social networking sites

    1996 Dirt style for, 120

    adding interaction to typesetting, 12

    changing rules of web design, 11

    generating video contests on YouTube, 116–117

    hobbyist designers creating, 107

    modularization and syndication, 117

Spatial Flash, 133

specialization, of professional web designers, 11

spectatormag.net, 102–103

Splash Flash, 133

standards, code vs. style, 13

starry backgrounds, 1996 Dirt style, 118

Steadman, Ralph, 168–169

stickers

    1996 Dirt style, 113–115

    Hand-Drawn Analog style, 170, 177

Stone, Jordan, 134

streaming video sites, Fullscreen Fashion style, 164

structure, text as, 59–64

style, importance of web design, 181–185

    craft of, 185

    function following form, 184

    importance of web designers, 182–184

    malleability of web, 182

    usability experts and, 184

subtractive, ink colors as, 73

SuperTiny SimCity style, 7

surfing, in Corkboard Sprawl style, 125

surrealism, Fullscreen Fashion style

    influence of, 142

    landscapes, 156–161

    uses of, 162

Swiss grid, 48

Swiss modernism

    Late(st) Modern style and, 44

    of Wolfgang Weingart, 45–47

syndication, 1996 Dirt style, 117

T

taxonomical design categories, 15, 18

technical perspective, web design from, 18

technological topics, Dot Matrix style for, 104

templates

    Blogger, 110

    for hobbyist designers, 107

    Indexhibit layout using, 31

    MySpace, 110–111

tex-server.org

    monospaced type, 94

    unbounded Corkboard Sprawl layout example, 128

text

    Fullscreen Fashion style site depth, 154–155

    Fullscreen Fashion style using unobtrusive, 141, 143, 151–153

    Hand-Drawn Analog style, 172–174

    as structure, 59–61

    as texture, 57–59

text-centric design styles, in this book, 17

texture

    in Dot Matrix style, 94–97

    in Hand-Drawn Analog style, 176–177

    text as, 57–59

theartgalleryofknoxville.com, 131–132

thegoodthebadandthequeen.com, 138–139

theonion.com, 164

threadless.com, 174–176

Times New Roman typeface, on old school sites, 32

tocame.com, 151

BUILD YOUR EXPERTISE,
ONE TECHNIQUE AT A TIME

Why sort through piles of documentation when you can focus on the techniques you most need to learn?

How-Tos books focus on those features you're most likely to use, showcasing each in a clearly explained, well illustrated, stand-alone technique, complete with a relevant tip or two.

Adobe Dreamweaver CS4 How-Tos:
100 Essential Techniques
ISBN 0-321-56289-5

Adobe Fireworks CS4 How-Tos:
100 Essential Techniques
ISBN 0-321-56287-9

Adobe Flash CS4 Professional How-Tos:
100 Essential Techniques
ISBN 0-321-58004-4

Adobe Illustrator CS4 How-Tos:
100 Essential Techniques
ISBN 0-321-56290-9

Adobe InDesign CS4 How-Tos:
100 Essential Techniques
ISBN 0-321-59094-5

Adobe Photoshop CS4 How-Tos:
100 Essential Techniques
ISBN 0-321-57782-5

Adobe Photoshop Lightroom 2 How-Tos:
100 Essential Techniques
ISBN 0-321-52637-6

Visit **www.adobepress.com** today!

Adobe**Press**

Be inspired—open a New Riders Voices That Matter book today!

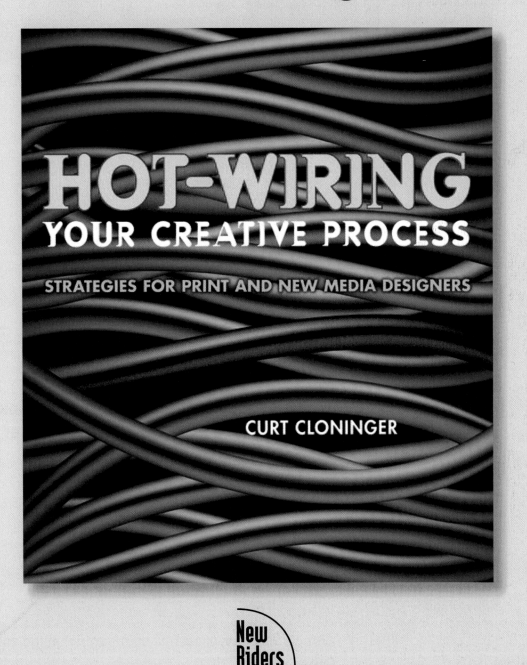